ALSO BY LLOYD HOLLIS CROOKS
Grenada Ghost, a murder mystery

ICE AND EYES IN THE SUN
True Love Comes Late, Sometimes

A True Love Story
by Lloyd Hollis Crooks

Published by
Wayne Brathwaite Publishing
519 East 26th Street
Brooklyn, New York 11210
E-mail: crooksgg519@aol.com
Ph: 1-718-693-7610 / 1-646-265-3239
www.lloydholliscrooks.com

Copyright 2000, by Lloyd Hollis Crooks
Published 2014

All Rights Reserved. No part of this true story may be reproduced, stored in a retrieval system, or transmitted, in any form, or by any means, electronic, mechanical, photocopying, recording, except for the inclusion of brief quotations in a review, without the prior permission of Lloyd Hollis Crooks.

Library of Congress Control No. 2014903679.

ISBN 0-9666296-3-9

Printed in the United States

Front cover art: Nathalie I. Thébaud

Book designer: nkkoprinting@gmail.com

This book is dedicated, posthumously,

To the Three Queens:

Enid Cynthia Bain-Crooks
Mary Louise James
Felicita A. Raynor

Block Watchers of East 26th Street
(between Flatbush and Foster Avenues)
Brooklyn, New York 11210

Every caregiver for an Alzheimer's disease patient should read this true love story, *Ice and Eyes in the Sun--True Love Comes Late, Sometimes*. This story tells how families fight among themselves but in times of adversity they band themselves together in love. My heart saddened when Lloyd broke down in tears because he could not play on the piano *My Funny Valentine* for his wife, Enid, on Valentine's Day. She was in the last stage of Alzheimer's and could neither walk nor talk. Once she sang as a nightingale, and he accompanied her on the piano in church. To watch Lloyd, the womanizer, become a caregiver with love and tenderness for his sick wife is a social act that should be documented in Wikipedia's Amazing Acts of Humanity.

Nigel K.C. Crooks

Crooks's writing is awesome. The dialogues in *Ice and Eyes in the Sun--True Love comes Late, Sometimes* are terrific, humbling, apologetic, sometimes racy. It is about the confession of a man born in sin and shaped in infidelity. He becomes the caregiver for his wife, dying from Alzheimer's disease, and for the first time in their 53-year marriage, he tells her that he "loves her truly." A great love story! I am warning you: Keep a box of Kleenex nearby to blot your tears.

Anita Scanterbury

A great love story written in the style of Toni Morrison's *Beloved*.
Collis DeCoteau, A Place Called Gouyave

I see my life in *Ice and Eyes in the Sun--True Love Comes Late, Sometimes*. The only difference in my case is: My man is dead, and I am alive still weeping for his love.
Ruth B.

Never have I read a true love story so unfiltered. At times I would choke Lloyd if he were close to me. I'd do the same to Enid. But at the end of the story I want to hug them for their humanity burst out like ceremonial cannons from the fort on me.
Gail Crick, MSW

For Fats whose voiceless prose taught me what true love is.
Lloyd Hollis Crooks

"Love cannot be expressed on the outside until it flows from within."

Austin H. Tuitt
Pearls of Inspiration

ICE AND EYES IN THE SUN
True Love Comes Late, Sometimes

A TRUE LOVE STORY

ACKNOWLEDGMENTS

All my life people have shown me the way when I was lost at the crossroads or when I was equally confused on the straight and narrow way, and I thank those caring souls. There are others who have helped me, financially, psychologically, clinically, sociologically, and physically; and I thank them, too.

Two men have helped me, physically; they are always at the fore of my memory and have my everlasting thanks. They are Mr. Percy and Mr. Marshall, my neighbors, in my hometown Fyzabad, a little oil town in the Republic of Trinidad and Tobago. They have saved me from drowning. I was ten years old. I went to fetch water from the deep well for my mother to cook. The weight of the water in the oversized bucket tied to a piece of rope pulled me down when I tried to pull up the heavy bucket to go home and boast of my strength to get my mother's two-word praise—"strong Blackboy." (That's my mother's pet name for me). I went down twice, swallowed water, and bits of lilies. Before my third descent in that deep well, I struggled to stay afloat but to no avail. I had given up hope of getting my mother's praise again. Then up came my two heroes who dashed off their bicycles, pulled me out the well, and saved my life.

There are two more people I had forgotten to thank in my first novel, *Grenada Ghost*, and I am now taking the opportunity to do so. They are Mavis Davidson and Jean Remy who accommodated me in their one-bedroom apartment till I got a place of my own. I had come to Brooklyn for the first time on a very cold night in an onion-skin jacket after a tiring British West Indian Airways trip from the Republic of Trinidad and Tobago, West Indies, to JFK. Mavis and Jean's never-forgotten kindness happened because the friend who had faithfully promised to accommodate me reneged on her promise, without prior notice. I was drowning on land with the weight from the coldness, in and out, of my flimsy jacket; and my chattering teeth were unable to talk to ask for help. Up came those two godsends. Thank you, Mavis and Jean, my BFFs.

The writing of this true story, *Ice and Eyes in the Sun—True Love Comes Late, Sometimes*--took me 15 years to complete. It speaks of the protagonist, my wife, Enid, an Alzheimer's disease (AD) patient, who never received my love and affection because of my pathological womanizing ways. But when she was in the final stage of AD, and I thought I would die from prostate cancer, my love for her was fathomless, and I became her loving primary caregiver. Other caregivers in therapy with me have helped me find the right words and compassion to complement my text—and I thank them.

In the medical field, my sincere gratitude goes to Dr. Avidah H. Rudberg, my and my wife's urologist, and his staff—Dr. Igor Chan, Nina Rudberg, office manager, Luba Goncharuk, medical assistant, Ina Kunnin (no longer in his employ), medical assistant, Galina Flom, secretary, and Emma Goldenberg, sonographer. Dr. Rudberg, with his puckish smile, subbed as a standup comedian to alleviate my fears before my prostate procedures. His clinic is in Little Odessa, Brighton Beach, Brooklyn; and he is a very good surgeon.

Dr. Ramaswami Sundar was Enid's first neurologist, but Dr. Howard A. Crystal was her neurologist until her death. We need more doctors with their empathy and humanity.

Enid's internists, Dr. Lalasa Valasareddi, Dr. C. Swaminathan, and Dr. Michael Onorato Davia have my heartfelt appreciation and thanks for their attention to her.

I owe a debt of gratitude to Dr. Andreas Adams and Lorna Walcott-Brown, MSW, counselors, for group therapy classes for caregivers at Downstate Medical Hospital annex, Brooklyn, for imparting their knowledge on where caregivers should go to get help to alleviate that extra stress. Dr. Francois Elder Thébaud, my friend, gets my thanks for giving me permission to use an excerpt from his book, *West African Mental Health—Practitioner's Guide*. Patricia DeCoteau, RN, BA, was like my *Merck Manual of Medical Encyclopedia*. I called on her constantly to explain medical terms. Thank you, Pat. Thank you, Dr. Kordai I. DeCoteau for pointing out an overlooked medical error when proofreading *Ice and Eyes -- True Love Comes Late, Sometimes.*

Enid's siblings, worthy of mention and praise for their concern for their sister, are Pearl Roach, Dr. William T. Bain, Versil Ferguson, her husband, Neville Ferguson who came to Enid's funeral; and Glynis Bain, Enid's niece, who did research for me.

Joanna Haye was always with a smile no matter

how stressful the task of part-time caregiving and college studies at York College. She always dolled up my wife pretty, and she was there when my wife had her first seizure. She called 911. She has since attained her Ph.D. in molecular biology at Princeton University. Georgia "Prophetess" Haye, secondary caregiver, always said, "Mr. Crooks, you are not Superman. Stop helping me! Go away when I come to work." I thank you, Prophetess, for working overtime without compensation. Thank you, Herman Scanterbury, Enid's best buddy, who amused her when she was lucid, and his praying-mantis wife, Marion, whose prayer meetings Enid attended and loved even though she knew not why she was there. Eleane McKenzie, the last secondary caregiver, was a great help to my wife, and she showed interest in her work. Thank you, Eleane. Elizabeth "Sis" Griffith knows about the behavior of AD patients because she works with them. She had forewarned me that my wife's physical appearance would deteriorate, but I should never stop loving my wife because of her appearance. I thank you, Sis, for those words of advice. Thanks, Ezla Phillips, for always inquiring about my wife; and praise and thanks to Janice Longmore, RN, for helping me during hard times; and for telling me what is likely to happen to us when we don't stand up for social justice: "The boomerang will come our way." Thank you very much, Elender "Lady" Jones, for all your loans, without interest, when I was dead broke, and for helping me with Ezlon.

Janet Williams, though blind, taught me how to discern if a caregiver is unkind to Fats. Fats is Enid's nickname. I applied Janet's advice and came home unexpectedly one day and found out that the secondary caregiver that I had trusted most was really the Devil's wife. I found my wife's head stuck between the bed and the wall. I thank you profusely for that advice, Janet. It was a red-letter morning when I fired "that f****** bitch," as you rightly called her.

Dwayne Arbuckle helps all the senior citizens on the East 26 Street block (between Flatbush and Foster Avenues), Brooklyn, New York. He also brought pampers for my wife. Thank you, Dwayne. Elder Austin H. Tuitt, community organizer, artist, and boyhood friend, allowed me to use an excerpt from his book, *Pearls of Inspiration*. I thank you, Elder T. Thank you, Alston "Jan" Noble, my oldest friend and brother in "good" crimes. He lent me his bungalow apartment *to court* Enid when she was my *new girlfriend*. Also, thanks, Jan, for travelling from Trinidad and Tobago to see Fats before her death.

This Good Samaritan, a man with a vision, has my countless thanks and praise. He saw Enid when she was in the middle stage of AD, sitting in her Buick in a gas station, late one night, because she did not know how to get home. He drove her home; and he refused my reward. I also thank the youngest Good Samaritan I know. He refused to tell me his name. He is the teenager who rescued my wife when she walked away from where I had put her to sit on the day of the West Indian Labor Day carnival in Brooklyn. He walked the length and breadth of Eastern Parkway till after midnight to find me. I felt my hot tears when he refused my compensation. I wish those two Good Samaritans overwhelming success for the rest of their lives.

Many thanks to my Fort Lauderdale buddies who chauffeured me around and dined me when I did my research on AD at Broward County, Main Library, Florida -- Gladys "What-the-Heck" Homère, Igor Thébaud with his wicked laughter that I've tried to imitate but never could, Gary Thébaud, Lisa André, Marc Pierre-Pierre, and his lovely wife, Nathalie I. Thébaud. She is the artist whose painting on cover page depicts women with "ice and eyes in the sun." Nicole "Niggs" Thébaud-Fox is the comedian of the Ft. Lauderdale gang, and she's on my pedestal. Niggs, may I say your help was invaluable, and I could never repay you in cash or kind. All I can say is "Thank you, dear friend."

It gives me great pleasure to thank Eulah Joseph who remained up to the end with her pastor and friend, Pastor Enid Crooks, at their church, Divine Truth Assembly. She is a "real" friend. Myles Raynor, Anthony and Harriett "Tweet" Turner, you are my best neighbors. You always shovel my snow, or trim my fence, without my asking for your help. I thank you very much for your continuous help over the years. Gwendolyn Clarke, who left a stone on my step to let me know that she was at home in case I needed help with my wife, I thank you very much, Mrs. Clarke. June Fordrass, my dear friend, you will never be forgotten. You sat in one day in the absence of the regular secondary caregiver. You and the Firemen of Ladder 157 (Brooklyn) have my thanks and praise. You took care of my wife when the conjoined building was on fire and smoke was getting into our house. You and the Firemen did the needful and prevented my wife from suffocating. June's husband, Donald "Uncle Dee" Fordrass, gets posthumous praise. He taught his nephews, the other teenaged boys of Gower's Well Road, Fyzabad, and me *how to make girls fall in love with us*. I thank you, Uncle Dee, for your sex education; but it got me in *big* trouble with Fats when I plastered my body with Old Spice as foreplay before sex.

Curtis Jackson frantically searched the suburbs of North Carolina for his mother-in-law when she walked away during her "sun downing" hour. His find ended my tears that day. Words are not enough to thank you, Curtis.

Florence Strauss, who has an eye for syntax, Anita Scanterbury, equally diligent, and so is Collis DeCoteau, the author of *A Place Called Gouyave,* and a griot of everything Grenadian. They willingly read the fortieth and final draft of **Ice and Eyes in the Sun**. I am thankful, guys, for your keen eyes and for correcting my editorial snafus.

My living siblings, Gloria Crooks, Merle Charles, and Steve Crooks, I thank you and love you very much. You have embraced me, loved me, and respected me as your big brother. People don't believe me when I tell them that we have never had a quarrel from since childhood. My deceased brother, Paul, you were "the greatest." I learned to give my children pocket change because of you. As an apprentice learning the welding trade in the oilfields, your salary was $15.35 bi-weekly. After you gave Mammy your sealed-envelope packet, and she opened it and gave you pocket change, you always gave me a pocket change from your pocket change. Wow! You made me happy: I had money for the ten-cent movies in pit, and I made noise to let everyone know that I was there.

My children—Judy-Rae, Kai Lloys, Taariq (my first proofreader), Gail Shelly-Ann, Nigel, Trish-Ellen, and Ezlon—I know you love me much, but I love you much more. And thanks for polishing your parents' life with style.

Nigel, you encouraged me to write this story because you thought it would be cathartic for me. And it was. When you all were small and got a dime for your allowance from me, we all sat around the dining table; and I had given you all an opportunity to critique my all-round behavior; but only Trish-Ellen, eight years old, did. She asked for an increase in her allowance and said, "Mammy and daddy, if I did not get an increase in my allowance, I will run away and join a gang." Now that you are all adults, you are free to critique my text—my parenting and my behavior as an unfaithful husband, without fear—and you don't have to run away from your gut feelings. Shelly-Ann, your caregiving help to your mother is not forgotten. Tariqua "Princess" Nehisi, my lovely granddaughter, I thank you for taking me to the doctor and other places when your father, my permanent chauffeur, was unavailable. Many thanks, Gerald Gibson, for putting your mother-in-law many nights in bed when I was unable to lift her because of my prostate procedures. Caleb "BJ" Gibson and A'dhayna "Charlie" Nehisi, if I had to pay for your computer help I would have been in debt up to my neck. Thank you very much. I will compensate both of you on your graduation from college.

Khafra "Bing" Crooks, I know you played rugby in South Africa, and soccer in Nottingham University, England. But in Brooklyn you wore other hats: grandson, proofreader, and my-unpaid-and-personal psychologist. You also alternated as the night nurse to Granny, and secondary caregiver-at-large. It's ineffable for words to express my thanks and gratitude to you, Bing. Your second tongue being Portuguese, you coaxed me to bed with your sugar fingers on the keyboard when you played Latin music. Your yeoman's service is indelible in my brain. Your Granny did not baptize you in vain. In group therapy, a soldier cried, "Caregiving for my mother is tougher than boot camp." Were it not for you, Bing, I would have had boot camp plus primary caregiving for Granny on my plate. Again, thanks a million, Bing.

For 18 years I sat every lunchtime with the girls,

my friends, at Sullivan & Cromwell, and they were all at Fats's funeral service; and joining them was also Senior Pastor Susie Elliott of Mt. Paran Baptist Church. Her church is an oasis in Bushwick in implementing HIV awareness. Thank all of you very much for remembering me and being there to share my sorrow. I also thank all the members of Divine Truth Assembly who turned out to say goodbye to their pastor--Pastor Enid Cynthia Bain-Crooks.

    Thank you, my friend, Nandi Keyi, author of *The True Nanny Diaries*. Every immigrant who has come ashore looking for dreams, sometimes achieving "derailed dreams," should read your novel. Senator Kevin Parker writes: "I enthusiastically support this seminal work of Nandi...." Nandi, you help rusty me to get my literature on the market again. Your kindness is supreme. It was a blessed day when I walked by your book kiosk when you took part in the Grenadian Parasol: A Literary Affair.

    To those who prefer to remain unnamed, and those whom I've forgotten to mention for giving me the hand needed to take care of my loving wife, Enid Cynthia Bain-Crooks, you are proof that **commununity always comes ahead of individualism.**

XXII   Lloyd Hollis Crooks

Ice and Eyes in the Sun

Lloyd Hollis Crooks

1

A split second late, the train would have sliced my new lover and me as we enjoyed romance on the train track. It was a night in August, 1959. A *new* lover *during those days* was the *best* woman to have, whenever, and wherever. I saw beauty and true love in the newness of the feminine flesh below me or on top of me, horizontally. That was my sick interpretation of "beauty in the eyes of the beholder." I had inherited that disgusting interpretation of what true love is from my father, whom I had loved and had worshipped in an unfathomable way. He never hid from me that he was an outlier to the love of one woman, probably he wanted me to follow suit having been jilted by the brown woman he had first loved and wanted to prepare me for the downfall in loving *only* one woman. He was nicknamed Tiger, and was born in September, 1910. But the insincerity of the future repaid me with my own tears when I, too, was jilted by a new lover, a vulgar woman, who blasted in public, "You are a lying, deceitful, conniving S.O.B. Your sex is soft like the dough man's. Christine told me that, too." I replied, "Sex was born before life so why not enjoy sex with my dough man before you die, bitch." I ran out of the supermarket where onlookers stared at me because I was afraid she might have said more horrible things about my sorry, sex life. Yet I lived for my infidelity and befriended women just as vulgar; and I continued to feed my ego that was as shallow as base boards.

My mother always told me from childhood that I was just like my father: "Beware of your future, Blackboy," she warned. She was born in 1908, and my love for her was lukewarm at times because of my excessive worship for my father. People in Water Dam, in the oilfield estates of TLL (Trinidad Leaseholds Limited), Fyzabad, in the then colony of Trinidad and Tobago, West Indies, my birthplace, hardly knew my father's Christian name. He was a part-time barman in TLL Sports Club, and he never drank alcohol. The patrons loved him, but loved his nickname more: "Tiger, bring me a beer. Tiger, pass me a shot of rum.

Tiger, when last you clawed your victim. Those drunkards laughed, gobbled shots of alcohol, and your no-good father laughed louder," my mother had told me when my father did not bring the three dollars he had promised for the maintenance of his three illegitimate children. When I delivered my father's eulogy, months short of his ninety-first birthday, I referred to him as "the loving Tiger," looked at women mourners with handkerchiefs on their eye lids, and then I forced myself to look one more time at the wreaths on his casket. But as much as I had loved him, it took years to forgive him because he did not marry my mother. My mother was jet black; and my father loved brown-skinned women.

That August night of 1959 when my lover and I were almost sliced by the train wheels, my father had made an unexpected visit to my new apartment to congratulate my wife, Enid, and me on our wedding, but I was not at home. Enid and I were five months married, and she was due in September with our first child, Judy. In those early years of marriage I came home late nearly every night, and I had lied about my lateness, except on nights when I worked late as a specialist secretary/

stenographer in the Office of the Prime Minister of the Republic of Trinidad and Tobago, Whitehall, the seat of government, and covered "sensitive" conferences. I also spoke the truth about my lateness when I was a reporter in Parliament, and the House and the Senate had late sessions on Budget Debates.

Hurrying home to see Enid when she was pregnant was the least of my concerns. During pregnancy, her night sickness was clockwork: At eight, she vomited and held the toilet bowl for support and her belly wobbled on the porcelain. She had told me of her nightly discomforts as I walked in from my haunts, but I barely listened to her: I only thought of the woman I'd just left and what we did in bed.

At nine o'clock, or thereabout, on that almost fatal night of August, 1959, when I had sex on the train track, my body was half exposed in lovers' cove, a high thicket, which bordered the train route. I felt the current of approaching trains and knew whether they carried passengers or cargo. Other lovers in the cove knew that current, too, and how to shift themselves in the darkness. I didn't get my usual dark spot in the thickets, so I chose the railway track for *making out*, forgetting TGR (Trinidad Government Railway) prompt schedule does not run on my impromptu sex schedule.

The locomotive headed west, its course parallel to the eastern corridor of Trinidad, and its destination was the railway yard in Port-of-Spain, the capital. The iron engine came around the bend of the bushy path of the town of St. Augustine that seats UWI (University of the West Indies, formerly the Imperial College of Tropical Agriculture), and no longer the home of Winifred Atwell, world-famous boogie-woogie pianist from whose opened window I heard her tantalizing music and prayed to be a pianist when I was nine years old. Mr. Harry was Atwell's neighbor, and I had spent Easter vacation with him. Sixteen years later I was again in St. Augustine, not listening to Atwell's music, but making love on the train track.

My new lover was a city girl in pencil skirt. She did not know how to deposit her sandaled feet in the darkness of St. Augustine hideaway, and she held me close for guidance. But she knew when the unpredictable dry river in Port of Spain would gush down, without warning, and would wash away everything within its path. Her gut instinct also told her when not to make shortcuts through the dry river to get to her house on Piccadilly Street. Piccadilly Street inhabitants then, and its environs east of the dry river, were called "Behind-the-Bridge People," a sociological put down by people west of the dry river—"We on this side are better than you over there" was an unwritten parlance expressed by their foreboding. My behavior to this pretty woman at my side was tantamount to the uncharitable behavior of the west side group. But my date could not have suspected my conniving because of my skillfully practiced deceit. Her lovely attire, and the way her body rubbed on me, made me momentarily ignorant of the train's schedule. I had forgotten that the westbound train would not stop at St. Augustine for passengers, and that I would not have sufficient time to finish my act on the track before the whistle blasted around the semi-circular bend. I knew the entire geography of the space between Tunapuna and St. Augustine because I lived at Tunapuna and traveled on the passenger train to go to work in the city.

  Suddenly, the train's headlight beamed, and its smoke moved in the opposite direction of its charging wheels. The whistle blasted twice again. I have since come to the realization that the engineman must have seen two people in imminent danger, and that's why he blasted the whistle in quick succession. He must have closed his eyes, sure that there would have been an impact of his iron machine on humans.

With both hands, and a cruel force, I pushed my date off the track and leaped with lightning speed behind her, but one of the protruding passengers' steps ripped my pants and cut the back of my left leg. As I write this account of the incident fifty two years later, I find myself touching the unevenness of that healed wound. I was too numb to feel the pain immediately on that August night of Nineteen Hundred and Fifty Nine or to speak to my date after our escape from death. She went her way, and I limped into a taxi. I lived a short distance away but it felt like a long ride home. I hobbled up eight treadles of steps to get inside the house owned by my mother-in-law.

"What happened to you, Hollis?" Enid shouted. She helped me from the third treadle. The child in her belly seemed to have dropped lower as I pressed on her shoulder for support.

"A crazy cyclist knocked me down on

Eastern Main Road, and he didn't even stop to help me," I said.

"If I had got hold of that (redacted) man I would have choked him to death." She cursed that invisible man all through the night as I groaned in pain.

She boiled water, cleaned my wound, and applied iodine to it. She was tender during her clinic, but my thoughts were on what could have happened on the train track to me and an innocent woman who thought I was "substance not knowing that I was straw instead."

It didn't take long for Enid to get hold of my constant lies and infidelity: She found out that I was not on any Government assignment but away for two weeks with a woman when our first child, Judy, was born.

"You are such a stink liar, but I will not wait until you or I die to forgive you," she said, with tears, with a depth of scorn for me, and pity for herself, as I remained mum.

Now Enid cannot rebuke me for my infidelities as she did in the past, or accept my sincere apologies for my lies and past indiscretions, because she is in the late stage of Alzheimer's disease (AD). She has no memory, and she can neither walk nor talk. I, too, have ailments. I have had three procedures for an enlarged prostate.

On Tuesday, September 28, 2010, at 3:01 PM, Dr. Avidah H. Rudberg, urologist, called me in his office, closed the door, and said: "I got your biopsy. I'm sorry to say you have prostate cancer...." I was speechless. "You are not going to die. I want you to do a bone scan before the operation."

"Dr. Rudberg, can I bring my son, Taariq, with me after you get the result of my bone scan? My children are already sad because their mother has Alzheimer's so I am not going to tell them that I have prostate cancer. Taariq will tell them."

Taariq came on my next visit to Dr. Rudberg.

Dr. Rudberg said—I believe to alleviate my fears—"Your son is the striking image of you. And your family behaves like a Jewish family." His last comment was because my daughter, Trish, calling from North Carolina, had interrupted him twice on the phone when he talked to Taariq. Trish wanted to know the answer to every question Taariq had asked him about me.

What a difference sickness and time make:

Enid continues to be my wife—I never expected that she would be my wife for 53 years knowing how little I had loved her. But now she's my *newest* and *only* lover, though she's melting like ice in the sun, without an ego, and unable to help herself in any form or fashion. But whenever I see the sun I see hope for both of us living many more years in happiness. When I was a boy, my brother, Paul, had told me that I should look at the sun before nine in the morning and after five in the afternoon to strengthen my vision and to give me courage and hope for tomorrow. Paul had studied yoga, by books, with Paramahansa Yoganda (sic) from India. I thought Paul's advice was rubbish then. But now I look for the sun every day. Seeing the sun reminds me that my wife could live another day under my care and my love. True love teaches me a commitment to her that I'd never known was possible. True love teaches me that Alzheimer's disease, that "brain thief," cannot drain the swamp of our love. And my renewed love for my wife reminds me that I must be at her side, "till death do us part."

In lucidity, Enid outwitted me, every time, "from wire to wire." She ingeniously elicited the venues of my trysts—it could be that I'd talked in my sleep as I'm wont to do. She clawed me with her nails, on the street, in our basement, and whenever she imagined I cheated. Sometimes her imagination was on target. I never retaliated, and she shouted, "Coward, why didn't you hit me back so I could call the police!" I took her blows without retaliation.

"Mr. Crooks, when last you had sex with your wife?" Our family doctor had asked in her presence.

I did not answer, and both knew why.

He wrote the prescription. "See me back in two weeks." War broke out on the doctor's step. The dirty side of her vernacular equaled the dirty side of a hurricane. I walked Brooklyn streets that night: the streets with hoodlums were safer than sleeping in our bed.

I had only told our grandson, Khafra, of that night on the railway track and of that morning in the doctor's office when he graduated from Nottingham University, England, and had come to live with us again. We had matter-of-fact discussions. He had asked for my advice, laughing, on how to handle his passion when he didn't have condoms, and how to treat a woman when he's not sure if he's in love with her. "Your heat and your decency will let you do the right thing," I answered. "Am almost 80, and my heat is out. The ball is now in your court."

I am ashamed of my infidelity in the past, and I am also ashamed of past disrespect to some women. I no longer fit in the "mold of indecency to women." I am respectful to every woman now. Even when I'm tired I offer my seat to women on the subway. Of late, their answers are: "Keep your seat, pappy. Am okay...No, no, uncle. So kind of you." It is so nice to repent and get women's kindness. Caregiving made me truly fall in love with my wife for the first time. And, for me, true love comes late, sometimes. Caring is love. I never heard our vows on our wedding day, but today my love for my wife is real, and I see reciprocal love in her eyes when I push her in the wheelchair through the narrow lanes of our house and feed her near the computer. I get the feeling that she is reading what I'm writing about her. And I wish "genome cowboys" could confirm that, with certainty.

Enid Cynthia Bain Crooks is my wife's full name. She was the self-appointed pastor of Divine

Truth Assembly, a non-denominational church she founded on May 29, 1988. Being the pastor of Divine Truth was the avocation she enjoyed most after she graduated from Logos Bible College. Not even her family got her attention above her church, except on two occasions. And on both occasions, her church was the centerpiece: She re-baptized Trish, our last child; and Khafra, our first grandchild, was baptized for the first time. Trish was already baptized by the pastor of her Spiritual Baptist Church. Enid left that Spiritual Baptist church after she sponged in the religious teachings of Dr. David Mendez, a Pentecostal professor at Logos.

"His lectures fill me like the Holy Ghost's. It is not *that* bunkum of *my* Spiritual Baptist pastor." She qualified her pastor's name with uncharitable adjectives. She hinted her intention of opening a church and be called Pastor Crooks. She hastened her wavering decision and opened Divine Truth when she quizzed her Spiritual Baptist pastor on the Bible, and she found out he couldn't read.

Khafra's baptism was a top family secret. That secret was not told to Lloys, who is Khafra's mother, and our second child. Lloys knew she would be away on a journalistic assignment, and said, "Mammy, Khafra should never be baptized because baptism serves no purpose to my child." Lloys and Enid also had unending feuds about what Khafra should eat. "And, Mammy, I'm warning you! Khafra should *not* eat beef, *only* chicken and fish."

When Khafra was five years old, he called beef "red chicken," and he called fish "white chicken." Enid instituted her food-name-changing course for infant Khafra, and she baptized Khafra when LLoys was out of town.

Mother and daughter's sincere love and senseless dislike for each other alternated in sickness and in health, and their acrid tongues that laced their enemies were fitting for Wikipedia notations for mother and daughter's guile.

Pastor Crooks had chosen Marion Scanterbury to accompany her to BCAT (Brooklyn Community Access Television) to air her sermon. Her sermon dealt with the influence of God on man. When she preached that sermon in church, she questioned the congregants, "How did God influence you today?"

She answered her question: "Today, and

every day, He guides my footsteps."

"Why did you take Marion Scanterbury to BCAT instead of Reverend Moore, your assistant pastor?" I had asked.

"Marion is my good friend; her husband is my best friend; and he repairs my church and my house. And, furthermore, Pastor Moore has a bad habit of preaching over whatever I say as if he knows the Bible better than everybody. I would never take him on TV to show off on me."

"Pastor Moore would not be showing off on you; he would be expounding God's gospel as the Bible has it."

She looked at me. I knew that look from courtship. That look showed I'm just as dumb as Pastor Moore, even dumber.

Marion was versed in the Bible but made it her duty to staccato "Amen" throughout her pastor's sermon. She was a teacher in the island of St. Vincent, but she applied present-day tact in Brooklyn, the borough of churches, to please her pastor. She knew Pastor Crooks's mercurial moods, her pastor's pompousness, on and off the pulpit, and Marion knew best how to maneuver between her pastor's moods. Pastor Crooks never invited Marion to BCAT again. She never gave me a reason, and I dare not question her judgment.

At the dinner table she and I enjoyed the meal I had prepared. I asked, "How was your BCATing today, Fats?" I gave her that nickname having a sexual connotation on the first day we met in 1956 at Fyzabad Post Office.

The table was worthy of photographs for *Culinary—The Caribbean—A Culinary Discovery*. She inhaled the Sunday aroma at **519**, the name for our house, and I repeated the question, "How was your BCATing, Fats?"

"Great!"

"Did you preach about how you spied on me?" I had asked that question before, and that question was an aphrodisiac for good times in bed. This time the question was like if she had caught me putting arsenic in her plate.

"Stay out of your stinking sluts' beds, and I'd stop spying on you!"

I felt the gauge of her anger, and we ate dinner in silence.

My thoughts traveled during that silence to her graduation from Logos and what she had said joyously. "Lloyd Hollis, one day the good Lord would have me preach His Word in Africa." She called both names when she was excited. She called none when she was annoyed; and when she was pissed, "You! You!" were my first and last names. When she buttered me for favors, my names sweetened marmalade jars--and I loved those names when we had unholy sex.

In awe of her past, I continued that thought of when Dr. Mendez presented her the Logos Graduation Diploma and shook her hand. It was her red-letter day. She talked, and talked: "Honey, one day before I die I pray God grant me the opportunity to preach in the Motherland. If given the opportunity, I'll even preach to empty benches in Africa because God said go preach to the byways and the hedges."

Before AD, her fire for the gospel was madness, without merit, I thought. She preached by the roadside and her voice echoed in the subway. Sometimes I was her only listener. She loved high heels, and they were an asset to reach the lectern in her church where her Bible lay above her prepared sermon, redlined at the beginning of each topic.

Her brand of "secular spiritualism" was

not to make profit from preaching. She devised ways for people to come to church. Her salary from Consolidated Edison covered some church expenses. She depleted her 401(k) savings: She bought a building, a church van, furniture, new fixtures, and a second-hand organ that functioned for a short time. As much as I hated parting with my piano, I gave it to the church, and she conscripted me as the musician with her *kind* of contract.

My thoughts at the dinner table brought back her cunning. "Sweetie, play the piano for the glory of God on Sundays, and you'll have my music at nights for the whole week." Bedtime was her favorite hour for bartering her sexual favors for my gallivanting time.

"Is that a Christian's smile or a trickster's, Pastor Crooks?"

"What do you think? Let me kiss my loving husband on the spot he likes best for seeing the better way and for coming into the paling of grace."

"If playing the piano brings me into the paling of grace, I haven't agreed yet to your contract, Pastor Crooks."

"You will agree. Just don't come to my church to look at women's backsides. Keep your eyes on the black and white keys only."

We laughed, hugged, and she slept in my arms. But throughout the night I wondered if I am in love with her. That thought took over 40 years to leave me.

I enjoyed the early years as the church's musician, and I taped her sermons, which were political at times: "I preach God's politics on earth to battle Satan's in all of us."

The silence at the dinner table ended when I blurted, "Why don't you close down that blasted church? You hardly have members. I believe you opened that church to tell your brothers and sisters in Trinidad and Tobago that you have clout in Brooklyn, and people listen to you as their pastor. When would that sibling rivalry end? Are you all still fighting for your mother's properties?"

Her face muscles quivered. Her secondary characteristics for denouncing humans like me shone. Her glare burned my pupils, and her voice pitched: "My church is to praise God and to get a whoring devil like you anointed." She paused. "And, as for my brothers and sisters, keep their names out of your blasphemous mouth. I'm warning you! You know I hit back hard...and nasty!"

We went full blast, and nasty, at each other's reply. Our quarrels were constant when she was lucid. Discussions on institutions of socialization—family, religion, race, her *kind* of economics, her *route* to getting favors from politicians—"I voted for Republican George Pataki because another pastor told me Pataki would help churches in Brooklyn, and Divine Truth will benefit." Our family discussions always ended with quarrels, and I, as an outlier to fidelity, got her blue tongue for my infidelity.

Our early marriage was like pitching a crystal marble, from close range, into a small ring with clustered marbles to hit any marble as your target to get a prize. Any marble you hit made you a bull's-eye winner. Enid's philosophy was: "Just take the damn prize without questioning, 'Did I really win?' In the first place, the concessionaire never wanted you to win." She was that kind of concessionaire. Never question her integrity. If you did, she reproached you about her good deeds rendered as if there were no reciprocal kindness from you.

With a "vacant mind," Enid is still a "romantic chaos" by the way she speaks with her eyes. I answer with a new touch to her breasts as if it is the first time I've touched them, and she soothes my emotions with a look. Her attitude makes me find laughter for tears, and I think of my own mortality. "Thinking becomes a new experience" for handling leaps of her disease from stage to stage. I gaggle, at times, as a hapless goose, imagining our fate and our future--she with AD, I with prostate cancer, type 2 diabetes, high blood pressure, and a suspect heart that sent me to Lenox Hill Hospital and Kings County Hospital to have it checked.

We are 77 years old, and I did not celebrate our golden anniversary because I would have wept all through that celebration because I did not give her the love she deserves. Sometimes my mind slipped into the thought: *Would Fats have cared for me if I were the one with Alzheimer's disease?* Then I answered: *She would have done the same, and more. Nor would she have abandoned me, as I did to her, in the middle stage of AD.*

I did not understand her disease then. The spontaneity of clear thoughts was lost in an instant when I left her alone in the house for two months in the middle stage of Alzheimer's. We had been married for 39 years when I left.

Bunked in a rented basement, I enjoyed my new-found freedom from caregiving, and I returned to debauchery. But the golden rule, "Do unto others as you would they should do unto you," visited my conscience, ruled my thoughts, and reminded me of my responsibility to my loving wife, especially now that she's sick and needs my help. I returned home to take care of her.

Voicing my wife's *Alzheimer's story*, with my interchangeable roles—caregiver, surrogate, cheating husband—I'm reeling out facets of her hubris, humanity, and humor. Her life was once a drumbeat, on time, and never in "a cone of silence." When I came home late from my haunts, she said, "I'd get even with a man between my legs, too." I laughed. "Only a fool would laugh at a woman's threat. And I know what I'm capable of doing, fool."

She has lost that spunk, her pomp-and-pride trademark that once distinguished her as "a bitch" by her detractors, "nice lady," by block watchers, "Pastor Charity," by homeless men she fed in her church, and "straight shooter," by a Small Claims Court Judge. The judge had settled a payment dispute, in her favor, with an electrical contractor who wired her church.

Her "sense of mutuality" that evinced speed of retort and matched the opposition's insensitivity, with humor, or incivility, is no more. Her physical intimacy, that bathed me in eroticism until my genitals were satisfied, is kaput. Her G-strings, thin as air, that suavely left her legs and floated freely in her bathtub of foams and fragrances, an act of practiced coquetry, is no longer her game. She was always the round character in family dramas; protagonist or antagonist, her drama prevailed--in Mozambique it shocked the President.

Joaquim Alberto Chissano, the President of Mozambique, discussed Enid's Alzheimer's disease with me. She and I were his and Lady Chissano's guests on the occasion of our children's wedding in 1997. Lloys married their first son, Nyimpini. (*Nyimpini* means born in the struggle.) The first wedding took place in Maputo, in St. Stephens Anglican Church, and the Bishop officiated.

There were two wedding ceremonies, and Enid wore a beautiful dress at each ceremony. I couldn't help thinking something would go awry at one, or at all of the banquets. She was scornful, but her intolerance for people with bad table manners became dreadful as her AD advanced.

At a buffet luncheon, a guest picked up an olive from the dish on the table with her fingers, put the olive in her mouth, then she picked up another olive with the same fingers.

"Use the toothpicks on the table, not your dirty fingers, woman!" Enid said with rage.

The woman stepped out of the line and went way behind us. Later I learned that that guest was the wife of the doctor who delivered Nyimpini at birth. The President, his family, and other guerrillas in the struggle for Mozambique's liberation from the Portuguese, then hid in another country in Africa. The doctor, also a guest at the wedding, befriended us. He invited Enid and me to his home (I would not say where his home is). He said, "Lloyd, my country has the greatest game reserve in the world, and I would like you and your wife to see it." As much as I was willing to seize the opportunity, I declined. I imagined his wife, in her house, would have to watch her table manners because of Enid. Worse still, I would be sitting on needles and pins waiting for Enid's lectures to her hosts on whatever came to her mind. Alzheimer's behavior is impromptu.

The *Xiguiane* (second wedding ceremony) was a cultural fanfare. We had never witnessed such a joyous celebration. In my birthplace, Fyzabad, Hindu weddings were festival-like, and I had attended them, uninvited, to see when the bride's family paid the bridegroom to eat. I loved when the bridegroom refused to eat, and he was paid more money to eat. But nothing, to me, compared to the *Xiguiane* in Mozambique: A loving stream of matriarchs of the bridegroom's family waved palms and branches of trees and welcomed our daughter and her husband in Maleheice, the President's childhood hometown.

I addressed the village in English and told them why I gave Lloys to be married to Nyimpini. The President and the Mozambican Consul to New York interpreted my speech in Portuguese.

There was a sudden burst of merriment. The bridegroom's family, people of the *Shangaan and Maconde* groups, danced and sang *Xiku tsigua! Xiku tsigua!* Maria, Presidont Chissano's sister, explained the reason for their song and dance. She said: "There is a flock of birds in this country with shifting moods. If a strange bird, accidentally, strays into their flock and they hate that stranger, they'd pick it, even to death, in some cases. But if another straying bird flies into that said flock, and they love that new stranger, the flock will *welcome* it. And the flock will dance and sing *Xiku tsigua! Xiku tsigua!* That's their welcome chirp. We are glad to have your daughter in our family. That is why we are dancing and singing *Xiku tsigua! Xiku tsigua!*"

Enid's eyes roved on boys, perched on trees, as they watched the ceremonies. In the last ritual, her pupils never left mine in the family powwow. The private get-together was held away from the mammoth crowd, and it paid tribute to the bride and bridegroom. *Only* the fathers of the bride and bridegroom spoke, and *only* senior blood relatives were invited.

We sat in a circle which represented that we are equals. The President made a touching speech. He spoke of his son's feat, among other achievements: "As a young pilot, Nympini's small plane crashed, and he maintained his composure throughout the ordeal until he lost consciousness...." The President made no mention that his son had a Bachelor's degree from an American university.

I spoke of Lloys's past and present accomplishments — a graduate of Columbia University with a Master's degree, a journalist by trade, a United Nations' employee, and stressed her organizational skills as her mother's. As familial as that gathering was—the bridegroom's maternal grandfather with scarification, rooted in tradition and culture—had I said something that Enid disapproved, she would have objected vehemently as if I were asking for my name to be put on her savings and checking accounts.

Her tantrums had flared before on another occasion. "The President did not invite you to go to his farm, so why are you dressing to go?" She had asked the bride's godmother. "You have no decorum," she had told another who had raised her voice when the President introduced himself to our friends who had traveled from United States, London, and Trinidad and Tobago to attend the wedding.

I was the happiest man in Mozambique when the roundtable discussion ended.

The First Lady kissed me and said, "We

are family now." The President kissed Enid. I didn't hear what he told her. He shook my hand, and addressed me, "*Maseve* Lloyd, good luck to our children." I replied, "*Maseve* Joaquim, good luck and happiness to our children." Before the ceremony began he had told Enid and me that "*Maseve* is the familial salutation in the Shangana language by which we would address each other instead of Mr. President or Mr. Crooks... *Vamaseve* is if we are addressing you and your wife together." Enid called the President "Papa." He is called Papa by his children, grandchildren, and Lloys.

But Enid found another name and description for the President when she was very angry.

Lost during a tour of the Palace with spacious halls, murals, and beautiful paintings, Enid's wrath became her pathfinder to know my whereabouts. She shouted, her voice unworthy of a guest who had been housed and fed, without cost, and even pampered by the President: "Hollis! Hollis! Where the hell are you? Why are you genuflecting to that short, African man, and letting him drag you around like a little boy and leaving me behind?"

My tongue became heavy. I dare not answer her. President Chissano, a proud *Shangaan*, "a gifted diplomat," smiled when he saw my countenance. He waited on her, held her arm, and I saw in his poker face that a dormant guerrilla still lives. He was "one of the leaders of the war of liberation against the Portuguese" so he knew how to handle Enid Cynthia Bain Crooks from Flatbush, Brooklyn, a vocal combatant without camouflage, on his turf.

The President visited us in the summer of 1998. Mindful of protocol, I did everything within my power to prevent an encore of Enid's behavior as in Mozambique. I made sure I was never out of her sight. I feared that in her worsening stage of AD, had she lost me by forgetting how to get to the living room—it happened before--her unforgiving tongue would have again blared in anger. I meant for the President's short stay in Brooklyn to go smoothly. At that stage of her illness I couldn't tell when her hubris ended and Alzheimer's began. There was no line of demarcation that separated her excessive pride from her disease.

"A man's story is always badly told," writes Mia Couto, the Mozambican novelist. Enid's story, before and after AD, even if *badly told* by me, would be sharing information with caregivers, whatever their cultural sovereignty or adversity, for they are the heroes and heroines to the "24 million people living around the world with dementia."

Her copious knowledge of the women of the bible was phenomenal. Abijah was her favorite. "I'm like Abijah. I have a whoring husband." She measured me with scorn as if I were the godless King Ahaz, Abijah's husband, whenever I came home late, and she had the deep suspicion that I was with my paramour. Whatever she learned at Logos was used as mnemonics, a way that made memorization easy, and I was her pitchfork for her memory—for good, and for evil. When on friendly terms, she used me as her first audience to test the effect of her sermon before she delivered it on Sunday. I told her the truth whether or not she liked my critique. Sometimes, she said, "The spirit told me to preach something non-biblical." She preached on current events, and obeyed the spirit.

"What spirit is advising you, Pastor Crooks?"

Her eyes said, *Don't you ask that ungodly question again!*

Her temper was never suppressed. When her arrogance was least, look out: You walked on a land mine if you stepped on her toes during early

AD. Her supervisor did. She worked for 26 years as a customer service representative at Consolidated Edison. In the early stage of AD, she had prayed with, and for customers, who were in arrears for electricity consumption. One morning she put a knife in her purse.

"Why that knife, Fats?"

"My supervisor said the office is not my church, and if I ever pray for people again, she'll have me fired. The knife is in case I get fired."

I coaxed her, and she gave me the knife *that* morning.

In her great moments of lucidity, she bolstered her self-praise, which she called *Confidence*. She looked at our wedding portrait hung in a sixteen-by-twenty-inch frame on the southern wall of our living room opposite a giant mirror that gives us an imposing dimension.

"What a beautiful bride." She gloated at herself.

"What about your handsome husband?"

"You? Handsome? Not even that soft string below your navel that you share with so many women."

I expected the immediacy of her digs. She didn't write praises or prejudices under pseudonyms. She said them, without forked tongue, in your face. She never made up a Benjamin Franklin's *Polly Baker Story* of untruths and veered from her bitter-sweet childhood that molded her steeled character of integrity. Her steel was never putty in her heyday.

The "approach-avoidance conflict," a conflict in which I was attracted to, and repelled by her ego, was constant. I hated her ego as I hated the castor-oil-and-pot-salt paste that my mother had rubbed with root vine that whitened my teeth. But, somehow, I needed Enid's brashness, as Brooklynites, lined up on sleet, craved hefty slices of Junior's cheesecake that satisfied their insatiable palates.

Enid's brashness or fights never kept my infidelity in check. Cheating, especially *three-is-company-in-bed* was sacred to me. I was truly an enemy of fidelity. And I couldn't blame my father for this addiction. I was born with it.

Enid chastisement of my father's character hurt, but that was her retaliation for my infidelity and for not coming back to her church to play the piano. "You are just like your father!" she said so often.

She wasn't totally wrong. I am my father's second child with my mother. He had children in other counties of Trinidad and Tobago. We looked as identical twins. Once I jumped back from the mirror when I thought I saw him. "Tiger smelled you in Miss Liu's hands before he owned you as his child," my mother had said when she was stressed and needed money to buy food for his three children. Miss Liu was the unlicensed midwife who delivered his children at birth.

I had told Enid about Miss Liu and about one of my father's tricks: "When I was about six, my father took me to a woman's house to play with her daughter, named Jill. My father warned me sternly, 'Boy, you must *play with Jill right*.' He was annoyed when I played dolly-house with Jill and had made up a bed on the floor for Jill and me to sleep. Jill was the mother of her doll, and I was the father of her doll. I didn't know what *playing with Jill right* meant, but as I grew older I unraveled the villagers' toxic parable as they washed and dried their clothes by Gower's well: Jill was my father's daughter. And I did play with her *right.*"

Enid never retired the stories I told her of my father, especially the *Jill Story*. She cringed when my father visited our newborn, put his nostrils with protruding gray hairs on them, and inhaled their scents to trace their bloodline. She measured women with the white of her eyes if they spoke to me. Claire, a classmate, who had shared her coconut cakes with me in primary school, treated me like a leper when in Enid's company. Claire didn't even look at me for fear Enid might think we had something going on.

Her jealousy became unbearable when she found out that I fathered a child after our last child, Trish. Yet our sex was divine, not my love for her. Her flared nostrils' breath was an aphrodisiac that roused my passion for sex. Her *café*-toned body, dented like an hour glass, in fashion-forward styles, will always be remembered. Her unswerving loyalty to me, a lying and cheating husband, baffled me throughout the years. But somehow I felt her yardstick for true love was to own me as her property.

We met In June 1956. I invited her to my parents' house, and taught her the song, *The Nearness of You*. Her voice raised goose bumps on my body. I was, and still am, a 2-bit pianist who never played the correct notes to a tune. But her exquisite voice complemented the wrong notes I played when I accompanied her on the upright piano. I studied her and said to myself: *Stay away from that woman. She'd be difficult to shake off if she falls in love with me. She'd want to control me, and I'm not ready for that. I'm not ready to settle with that jealous woman, and I don't really know if I really love her as I'd love Meena.*

Before the dye of a not-so-sure love affair was cast, I married Fats.

I was repelled by her "all-is-mine" way of sharing, a trait she never displayed in our courtship. Her rebuke stabbed like cold steel when I lectured, "Married people should say, *all is ours.*"

"Like Norman [France], money-craved businessmen, fleeing the Prussians," described by Guy de Maupassant, the fatter her savings got the more she suffered the *thought*, and she expressed that thought, "You will never get my money to spend on your women."

I don't know why I threatened to walk out of her life when she was lucid because she never budged at threats; neither why I squirmed at her descriptions of my women friends because it was her habit. She was tough as rocks imbedded in granite when I tried to knock my suggestions of family fairness into her brain after back-bending to her for so many years. "Stop trying to change me. You're not Mom or Father!"

Her parents were her models about how life should be lived. Father bowed to Mom's wills, always. But Enid's idol was her grandmother. She called her Gamma. The villagers called her Teacher Evie. Teacher Evie was a Spiritual Baptist pastor, and Enid lived with her until 11 years old. Gamma spoiled her rotten, and she adopted some of the ways Gamma handled domestic disputes with her neighbors, and with members of her church hierarchy. When Gamma died and Enid returned home to live with her parents, who disciplined her, Enid described those days as "the worst days of my life." Then in a second breath she said, "Father spoiled me like Gamma, but if Mom hadn't whipped sense and deportment into me, I don't know what I would have become—probably a whoring street woman."

Her plastics began with A, American Express, and ended with M, MBNA America. She probably had others hidden. She used them the way children used monopoly money. America's credit system was her blanket. Notes were placed in order of denomination in her worn-out wallet, and those green notes were her passports to happiness. Shopping was heaven. The ATM was her hereafter which she visited daily in the height of her Alzheimer's.

"The ATM was your wife's way of easing her pain of your infidelity," Dr. Kordai DeCoteau noted, in pencil, when she proofread my manuscript.

"I'd rather hold Jesus close," Enid said, the few times I outwitted her from getting the clicker. The clicker was her weaponry for switching from station to station in search of televangelists' hellfire. She said those televangelists preached, purposely, for me, "a repeating sinner." My TV appointments with Oprah and Monday night football by way of the clicker were times of frustration because she devised ways of concealing the clicker in my drawers as if I mislaid it there. When I found the clicker, she said, "I will look at Monday night football with you, but first let me see what they are showing on other stations." Her smile was convincing as ever. But I changed the subject about the TV control.

"You already have furniture, Fats. Why buy new furniture because it is on sale?" I looked at her. "That is why you never have money for the better things."

She countered, "You had lived in a dirt house. You were accustomed to sitting on bamboo chairs, so I don't expect you to know the good stuff."

"Mammy, don't say that about our father," our children intervened at times.

"Country boy, am I lying on you?" She would burst with laughter, would roll on the floor, and the household chorused below her pitch. I enjoyed those laugh-aloud moments.

Enid went ballistic when I suggested, once too often, "Since your name is on my checking account, and you know my pin number, my name should be on yours."

She gave me a quick look.

"Fats, in case of an emergency, don't you think I should know the pin number of your checking account? That shouldn't be a secret to me because I will be acting on your behalf."

"You stopped telling me secrets about yourself long ago so why should I tell you about my money which is *my* secret. 'Partnership is a leaky ship,' Gamma told me.'"

There was a reason why I had stopped telling her secrets, especially about my job when I had worked in the Office of the Prime Minister. And it was really *long ago*: In 1956, I was appointed specialist secretary/stenographer in the Office of the Premier (now Prime Minister) of Trinidad and Tobago. Dr. Eric Williams was the Prime Minister. I was investigated and sworn to secrecy because my job brought me in touch with "sensitive" information. Nonetheless, I had divulged a sensitive bit of information to her to boast about my job and my knowledge of the Prime Minister's background.

Fats, you won't believe this: Today I took dictation from the PM, and I read hot stuff from *Cabinet Minutes.* Did you know Dr. Williams is one of 'the world's foremost research scholars,' and he graduated with first class honors from Oxford University? Did you know he is the author of *Capitalism and Slavery*, and his thesis alludes that the slave masters didn't abandon slavery because of love for their slaves, but because of economics? Did you know he taught at Howard University in the United States?"

"Wait! Wait! Hollis, how many times do I have to tell you that I'm smarter than you? I went to SAGS (St. Augustine Girls' High School) and learned French, Latin, mathematics, and studied world affairs. You lived in Fyzabad, in the deep woods, without a radio, without electric lights, and you had to go to Gower's well to find dirty water to boil and drink. I had all modern conveniences in my house because my father was a building contractor. And you didn't go to high school! You went to a vocational school for dunce children, and you only learned that Pitman's shorthand stuff. You graduated as a stenographer. Congratulations! Stop boasting and tell me what the hell you read in *Cabinet Minutes*."

I caved in and told her.

When I left my hometown Fyzabad, the only secret I knew, and kept from investigating policemen, was where the numbers runners gathered and paid out the purse. I'll reveal that secret now because all the parties are dead: It was in the culvert, in the bush, opposite my mother's wood-and-dirt house. The *new* kind of secrets I garnered at Whitehall, the President's office, had an intriguing pull. I had to share the news with my *new* lover, Fats.

I did not know then that Fats hid nothing from her brother, William, senior by two years, nicknamed Willy the Tank. The Tank had graduated from Teachers' Training College, made a small salary, and had three children. He drove his 1955 Hillman Minx into the gas station and said to the attendant, in a loud voice, "Put in quarter dollar." Whenever he bought gas, I poked my face outside of the Hillman and choked on my saliva. Soon I became used to his quarter-dollar purchases, and a few times I paid the quarter dollar to his delight. But many days, I, too, had less than a-quarter-dollar in my pocket.

Unexpectedly, I visited their parents, Enos and Otterly Bain. And there was Willy the Tank exhorting secret information to his parents. He behaved as if he were the Minister without Portfolio for Trinidad and Tobago and divulged information that I had told Enid in confidence. Mom, an astute storyteller, spent her leisurely hours on her porch, two yards away from the public standpipe. And, sometimes, she greeted her folks from her porch with hot topics of the village. Father listened to his son as if his son were Gamalial, the teacher of Saul of Tarsus, and he, the Tank, was supported by a fulcrum with the capability for action. My heart pounded with fear because having worked in the Prime Minister's Office I knew how news traveled to the PM from unknown sources. I shuddered what would happen to me if Government found out my slipups.

As we argued in our Brooklyn kitchen about putting me on her checking account, I rehashed our marriage problems in Trinidad and Tobago, and I reminded Fats of when she betrayed my trust and told the Tank what I'd told her in confidence.

"You are not tired of bringing up that long-ago stuff?"

"No!"

"You had bragged too much about your job with the Prime Minister as if you were his full-time secretary. You took dictation from him as a pool stenographer, probably the most inefficient in the pool."

"So?"

"That is why I had told Willy."

"It was sensitive information! It was strictly confidential! You wanted me to lose my job, or go to jail?"

"Whichever option you had preferred, braggart."

Our back-and-forth replies were punctuated with obscenity.

I was not taken aback by her truthfulness. In fact, I expected it. In a mellow way, I changed the conversation to mundane things, and then I went back to an old theme: "Fats, are you going to put me on your checking account and tell me the pin? In case you get ill, I'll be able to handle your business. Your name is on my account. It is not a secret hidden from you." My words were tender as the first night I approached her for sex in Alston Noble's bungalow apartment. I had a key for his apartment.

"Hell no!"

"You are so selfish!" We cursed each other.

I had a perfect reason to stomp out of the kitchen and go meet my *new* date without trumping up a lame excuse for leaving home that late hour.

"I'd be up waiting for you, nighttime Romeo."

"Why not wait on the porch in your nightgown?" I laughed, vulgarly.

She was the reasonable partner in the union when I returned home in the wee hours of the morning with lipstick on my shirt collar and gave a dumb excuse for the lipstick marks on other parts of my person. Pretentiously malleable as kindergarten putty, she acquiesced to all of my demands. I could have asked her, and she would have given me, her eyes, as bait, to go fishing in the Atlantic. When she volunteered her body and did not ask me where I was that night till early morning, I should have known she had "an ax to grind," a hidden motive in view.

Or, at least, I should have known my wife, permanently paranoid, always had a trick, or two, up both sleeves, and believed every shadow near to me was a woman abductor, who waited to take me away from her. It was a dominant subculture that she developed because of my *then* serial infidelity.

"That early morning was like a lovely tune," as the lyricist writes.

Fats bathed me in eroticism. In a teddy, never worn before, trimmed with Bordello excesses, her guile—again, I believed I talked in my sleep--elicited the rendezvous of my last tryst. The cunning fox let me enjoy my sun dance for two weeks before the flood.

She was the flood.

The third week she caught me with my *new*

lover and meant to extract my lover's eyes and give them to me had I not defended my lover's eyes with every part of my body. She harpooned me with her finger nails, and her downswing, via her high heels, was better than any golfer's. It caught my tender spot. That was the said spot she had kicked the mugger. The mugger got her pocketbook but she was certain that she fractured his gristle.

Disguised with a blonde wig, she went into Kings County Hospital Emergency waiting room to see if the mugger was there to be admitted into the broken-gristle ward. The mugger was not there. Taariq had pity for me when I came home for his mother had already boasted of her deeds: "Boy, I beat up your father because he would not let me beat his ugly bitch."

The following night Fats prepared a sumptuous dinner, and her jokes at **519** flowed freely, but she knew I was in pain from her shoe heel. Maupassant, from my interpretation, behaved as if he were the final arbiter on women's guile and morality. He would have mistakenly matched Boule De Suif's foresight with Enid's; but had he befriended Enid, she would have been in his *Selected Short Stories*, Penguin Classics, for outwitting him and eliciting his hidden thoughts during their secret talks on subcultures.

In another night of our romance, I itched to tell her of Milly, my paramour, with the hope that I would end my relationship with one of her haters. Their hating was mutual. Her séance almost worked to get Milly's real name. Had I fallen for her trick she would have researched phone books and questioned women randomly about if they knew me.

Kinky sex was her game to elicit information. She had succeeded before, and I was determined not this time. Her foreplay honeyed me into a bee.

"Honey, didn't you promise to tell me something?" She unbuttoned her top and swayed. I grabbed her.

With one breast, a mouthful, I swayed with her on the bed. I mumbled, "You like it, Fats?" I called her pet name often when instituting sex or having sex.

"Honey, Honey, don't you have something else to tell me?" Her coquetry was thick.

"Let's get down, Fats, and do it first."

She jerked my neck, jumped into a tailspin

with fire like a shot-down World War II pilot over the Pacific, and shot her venom. "Your sluts are always calling *my* phone."

I checked my neck. It was still on my shoulder.

"I pay the phone bills!"

She went from topic to topic, mean topics. "I don't believe you only have one *outside* child."

"Only *one*, Pastor Crooks, and he doesn't live outside. You know his name, and you never liked him."

"Your other sluts must have killed lots of fetuses before you had time to smell them like your cheating father."

"You had abortions, too!"

"For you! Not for other women's husbands like your dirty women!"

I lived in constant fear of her temper and her readiness for battle, *wherever,* on the drop of a pin. In elementary school she looked for battles on the strength of Willy the Tank, and she bribed him with half of her meals to handle her Friday fights. And, in Brooklyn, to retrieve her money from pyramid bandits, she conscripted Taariq, her teenaged son, nicknamed Snake. He, too, had his fame. He had slugged the class bully at Midwood High School, and the principal and guards checked his fists and made sure they weren't razors. The principal called me in and told me, "Your son didn't start the fight so he would not be expelled."

While she praised Taariq for retrieving her money from "That thief," how she described the pyramid bandit who was her friend, I said, "Fats, I'm taking Trish to apologize to the shoemaker?"

"I would *not* apologize to that Russian, so why are you taking Trish to apologize to him? Trish told him that he is not a good shoemaker. She is a child and could see that that Russian gives Black people in the neighborhood shoddy work."

"He said Trish cursed him when she came to pick up her shoes."

"Were you there?"

"No."

"Then you don't know if what he said was true."

"You were there when Trish told the black Santa Claus that he's not a real Santa, and you didn't shut her up either."

"For Christ's sake, she was just four years old. A child talks what she hears and sees. She only sees white Santa on TV."

Our children confirmed their mother's integrity outweighed mine: "Mammy calls a spade a spade. Daddy, you equivocate even when there is no reason to doubt all problems couldn't be solved with laws, guns, or soldiers' boots on the ground." Nigel, our fifth child, was direct. He worshipped his mother.

Taariq and Nigel made me feel like a spineless amoeba, and I lacked the courage to speak about people who offended me. They boasted of their mother's strength of character, and she proved it: In 1971 Enid and I had put a down payment of $50 to tie the purchase on a 2-family house in Bedford Stuyvesant. Such down payment was common then. Enid shook the realtor's hand, and said, "I love this house. Could I have a word with the tenant in the basement? What's her name?" Enid asked.

"Sure," the realtor said and went and sat in his car.

Enid introduced herself to the tenant. "Miss. Williams, I hear you are a very good tenant." The realtor never told her that. "I'm not coming into your apartment because my shoes are muddy."

Her shoes were not muddy. "But I want to let you know that I will be your new landlord soon. Tell me what I'll have to repair in your apartment so I'll have my carpenter, Mr. Herman Scanterbury, attend to everything immediately."

"Mrs. Crooks, I took the landlord to court. The judge told me that this basement is an illegal apartment, and I can live out the money that I have already paid this landlord. If you buy this building and become the new landlord I'll be living out my time for the next couple years."

"What's a couple?"

"I'll have to check what the judge downtown told me. Wait let me show you the paper."

"I believe you. Thank you, Miss Williams." Enid walked to the realtor's car and put out her hand. "I want back my $50. Now! You didn't tell me about what the judge told that tenant in the basement."

He handed her the crisp bill.

I would have hemmed and hawed before I say a word to the realtor. I would not have thought of questioning the tenant. But she was a businesswoman like Mom and Gamma combined. Her style was in-your-face, forever confrontational, no guess work, no lies. My style was lies, and more lies, before and after marriage. I wanted to lie on my marriage application and say that I was "a Laborer" to hide my true identity because most of my girlfriends knew I was working in the Prime Minister's Office. Also, Enid and I attended Tunapuna Anglican Church, and I did not post our coming marriage in that church. I posted our marriage notice in St. James Anglican Church in a different parish. Still I was caught. As I walked by to go into the Prime Minister's office for dictation one day, an employee who worshipped at St. James Anglican Church, whispered, "You never told me you're going to get married." I pretended I didn't hear her.

Enid and I were married on March 28, 1959. She looked gorgeous. Her wedding gown with crisscross panels was a gift from Aunt Edith who lived in Brooklyn. My cream suit, dotted with a black bow tie, was swollen as a blimp from the breeze caught within its large knee space. As we exited the one-car parade, the wind drifted us apart. Even at that moment I didn't know if I were doing the right thing. I knew true love *from me* wasn't the reason why I was there because *true love to any woman was never my bidding.* Probably I was there to end the apogee of extreme condemnation by the old folks who badmouthed pregnant, unmarried girls. (Now that I'm a man I realize those old maids "lived in glass houses" and had worse skeletons in their closets.)

The wind disturbed her short veil, and I patted her black curls. Her imitation pearl necklace and gold slave-band bracelet clashed as unmatched accessories but they represented her taste for material things. Her love for gold and real estate was a culture inherited from Mom who advised, "Enid, when you have gold you can pawn it in a minute to buy food for your children, if they are hungry. And when you have land in any country, you own a piece of the globe."

Enid "drank deep" of Mom's advice.

She commandeered me to leave Trinidad and Tobago *soon* because of a policy decision of the Eric Williams Administration. The government had introduced payroll deductions for taxes, called PAYE (Pay As You Earn).

I was promoted from my job at the PM's Office. I became one of six Hansard reporters in Parliament. We recorded, verbatim, in shorthand, or in palantype, which is similar to stenotype, in 10-minute intervals, the proceedings of the House and Senate. One Friday I rushed home on the train, the best means of transport in Trinidad and Tobago, which was stupidly abandoned by the Eric Williams Administration. As I stepped into the house, I used my fingers and pulled a piece of hot, half-cooked chicken from the pot and cooled it on the roof of my mouth with saliva. The seasoning was still fresh in the meat. I rested down my briefcase, shouted, bits of seasoning flew from my mouth: "Fats, Fats, the PAYE Bill is passed in the House, and on Tuesday the Senate would also pass it."

She stared at me. "There's no lack of range" when it comes to her stares.

"Fats, PAYE is law. Government will be deducting their taxes monthly from our salaries. They are not waiting for year-end to take out what civil servants owe them. If we owe them more, they will take out more at the end of the year."

"You'll settle for that PAYE foolishness from that deaf man? (Prime Minister Williams wore a hearing aid but skeptics thought he wore it to trick the Opposition into believing he never heard their questions.) You'll let that deaf man's government take out their money before we touch it? Let's leave Trinidad and Tobago. With your background, the American Embassy would give you a permanent visa."

I looked at her quizzically.

"If you get a permanent visa to go to America, wouldn't you leave *this* county in a minute?" *This* sounded as filth.

"Sure!" But I was bluffing. I was just promoted to the post of Parliament Reporter, and I liked my job. The United States was only on my mind when I listened to *Voice of America* for jazz music.

She harassed me daily: "Did you go to Marli Street?"

I dragged myself over to the American Embassy on Marli Street, Port of Spain, and filled out the required forms. In less than four months I was granted a permanent visa. I had to call my bluff because I would not have been able to live, without torment, in our new house, built by her building-contractor father. *Only* America was on her mind. I wondered then if her flawed vision of reality was marred by her cousin Hector's visit. Hector became a naturalized American, had come on a month's holiday, and had brought a pair of shoes for each day he spent in Trinidad. Her sin was shoes, and Hector was the second Devil, I think, who tempted her into going to America where he got his shoes. The enactment of the PAYE Bill was the original Devil or the "last straw" that broke her reasoning of how government works.

    I caved in to her request. Better said, she always won because she was not handcuffed to any policy decision, person, or place. I worshipped the Prime Minister for his work of scholarship and thought his politics were good for the country. She called him a short-deaf-know-it-all man and was about to reveal something that I had told her about his policy. But I screamed, and she didn't say what she was about to say. "Hollis, you got the visa so let us leave this country."

    I left for the United States in April, 1968 and soon thereafter Enid and our five children migrated from the Republic of Trinidad and Tobago, a country that supplies the United States of America two-thirds of its LNG (liquefied natural gas) joined me. We were 34 years old when we settled in Brooklyn, the fourth largest city in the United States that we love dearly and have never left. We were 42 years old when our last child, Trish, was born.

The cultural shocks in this great country were enormous. "Fats, you made me leave my good job in Parliament to come and mop warehouses in Brooklyn."

"You already have a job at Chase Manhattan Bank. God gave you the mopping job to get $25 each night to help feed your children. God is looking out for us, and better days are ahead."

Better days came. She no longer shopped in Pitkin Bargain Center, and I no longer mopped giant warehouses at nights. She shopped at Macy's. Jobs were advertised everywhere. In my first job at Chase Manhattan Bank I was promoted to *Troubleman* and covered all the items in difficulty and dealt with the traders. I lied to my boss and told him that I had to go to Trinidad and Tobago for my mother's funeral, and I didn't know when I'd return. He said he'd keep my job for me. I never returned and changed two jobs after I left Chase. Enid changed jobs, too. Her best friend, Myrtle Stuart, changed five jobs in one year.

We enjoyed our new life. Our children's thirst for education made us happy, and I praised

Enid for her decision to come to America. We lived a slow, success story. But I was advised by Marian Sutherland, Enid's cousin, who migrated to America over fifty years before us, "America is less racial than when my parents brought me here, but you and Enid should *never* talk success stories in front of your bosses. My father was fired for doing just that. He told his boss he went on a trip back to Trinidad and Tobago after 20 years, and his boss thought he was boasting over him." Marian's advice did not fall on deaf ears.

    It dawned on me one day to ask the question I always wanted to ask my wife. "Fats, do you get pay slips from your employer?"

    "I am not an illegal alien. Don't you?"

    "Yes. Mine has payroll deductions. Yours?"

    "I have a real job at Merrill Lynch! What do you expect?"

    "Have you thought that PAYE, which is *pay as you earn*, is another word for payroll deductions?"

    "What's your point, Hollis?"

    "You cursed the Eric Williams Government in Trinidad and Tobago because they introduced PAYE to get their taxes up front, but I didn't hear you curse Merrill Lynch for taking out United States Government's payroll tax deductions up front."

"You wanted me to take the fishing boat at night and travel contraband to Venezuela with Uncle Russell?" He was her mother's brother.

"I don't know what kind of tax system Venezuela has. I believed you tricked me to come to America to buy shoes."

"That's your problem if you got tricked!"

"You are so smart." My sarcasm was thick.

She looked at me as a fool, and I ended the conversation.

What a difference time and Alzheimer's make in my lovely wife's life.

Alzheimer's gradually, and clandestinely, crept into Enid's brain, and I could see her losing her smarts and wished it were not so.

Ezlon, my son, her stepson, helped her some days find her way home before he left for the Navy. He served proudly for six years on "USS" Kennedy. At graduation from boot camp, he was one of the flag bearers of the color guards. The Chicago wind blew the flag in his face and blocked his vision, but he didn't miss a step nor put the group's formation out of sync when they were retiring the colors.

He came into Enid's life in his teen years and at times their relationship was badly strained. When her illness worsened, he had accompanied her to the park and had held her hand. It was a Kodak moment with the yellow roses in our garden in the background. The only time I saw a similar scene that perked my joy was when a senior citizen with his cane danced with his wife in a wheelchair in Hollywood Beach Center, Florida. The Atlantic Ocean in the backdrop made a perfect picture for that Floridian couple. Nicole Thébaud, Gladys Homère, and I spent the evening on the beach. We spoke of that aged couple with disability, how true love is their reason for their longevity, and how true love comes late, sometimes. But as we spoke of the Floridian lovebirds, the way Enid and Ezlon had held hands crossed my mind as I looked out into the ocean. Joy relived, is fresh joy, tastier than before. But then I wondered if Enid knew who had held her hand.

Enid couldn't find her way home but she could still dance. And we danced at home at nights. Her cadence was precise when she danced with President Chissano at our daughter's wedding.

Soon she became unaware of all the niceties of life. Her steely resolve that I once feared became tempered putty.

She is now the metaphorical **ice in the sun**, without density, and I always look at the sun for strength. I watched ice that melted, and I'm watching it now—my faithful wife. She is like the solid block of ice that was pulled with pincers by muscular men from the ice factory and melted when left in the sun. As an office boy I had worked at Jaleel Aerated Factory in San Fernando, South Trinidad. Jaleel was the concessionaire for Joe Louis punch. I had gone with the icemen into an ice factory in Port of Spain, in the north, to purchase ice. On our way back to San Fernando, the truck broke down and the solid blocks of ice that were wrapped in crocus bags stayed longer to melt in the sun, but it melted as time went by.

Another comparison for my wife's deterioration was when my mother sent me to Mr. Metro, the only ice vendor in Fyzabad, to buy four cents ice. I returned with the ice in the blazing sun in my stepfather's food carrier. My mother protested, "Take back that little piece of ice to Metro. That is not four-cent worth."

Back and forth with the ice in the sun—at

times I try to look up at the sun to see if I could block its rays with my cap to prevent the ice from melting as I rolled my bicycle wheel, barefooted, on the hot pitch—I could no longer tell when the ice was four-cent worth from one-cent worth. But, comparatively, whatever is my wife's worth, it is priceless. I am her crocus bag and umbrella of care and true love trying, in my unscientific way, to delay her melting. With the help of cutting edge medicine and Government's Medicare I will shade her as long as possible from the destructive rays of Alzheimer's disease. I will continue to look at the sun for strength as my brother, Paul, had taught me so that I will have strength to take care of my wife.

Her pastime was to pull the hem off her dress, and fix the seams with her trembling fingers. She can no longer do such thing because she keeps her hands crossed on her chest. It was once fun and sadness rolled into a packet when I had watched my wife's characteristic no-needle-no-thread routine as if her sewing of the seams was to bedeck Cleopatra. But in her days of pomp she'd bedeck herself in the outfit first and then hand it down to Cleopatra. Buying clothes to match countless pairs of shoes was "her thing." Before she tried on a dress in any fitting room, she mumbled, "I hope nobody had tried on this before."

Now I dress her without her comment. What a difference time and Alzheimer's make. The once woman of steel is now soft putty. Her puttied self had its purpose: It stopped my dam with no water of love for her. Now my love for her is fathomless, and I feel the aliveness of her unspoken word of thankfulness and love for me each night I wheel her into our bedroom, put her in bed, and kiss her goodnight. The wheels of her chair are rubber, unlike the train's that almost sliced me in 1959 when she was pregnant. I am on the caregiving track, day and night, and I don't have to leap for my wife's safety or mine, even if the wheelchair runs over my bunions or drags off my wife's slippers.

2

Neither our courtship nor our shotgun wedding had telegraphed our fate or our future. Enid believed in the institution of marriage. Her father and mother were married and led an exemplary life for their six children to follow. My father left my mother with three children and married another woman.

Fifteen years after our marriage we went on our belated honeymoon in the Bahamas. Our honeymoon could be renamed *Spleens Honeymoon.* We chewed and ground each other like an ill-functioned rice mill that did not separate the rice for consumption from the stalk for compost. Our tolerance was molten into riotous arguments in a two-star hotel.

Rain poured. Our bedroom was blue and cramped with our luggage. The raindrops' patter was musical. I slapped Old Spice on my 125-pound frame as often as the raindrops fell. I was shirtless. My pair of pajamas was worn as a loin cloth. And my mind roamed. I don't know why my mind roamed, alternately, into my boyhood, and into another woman's bedroom, when Fats undressed.

She had day-dreamed of this one-day-it-will-happen honeymoon. When we got married we didn't go on a honeymoon because we were dead broke, and we lived at her godfather Victor Skinner. In fact, two weeks before our wedding she didn't know where I was. I was off the mainland as a secretary assigned to the Civil Service Regrading Commission. She also didn't know if I would return on the day set for our wedding. Her other deep concern was I would obey my mother who objected to our wedding. In the Bahamian bedroom she knew where I was, and the job of satisfying our carnal desires as honeymooners was a safe bet. She was eager to feel my liquid heat, and I was ready to enjoy her tenderness as when we first met and made love in Noble's bungalow bedroom. The expatriates from England who worked in the oilfields had lived in those bungalows before they returned to England. Now those bungalows are apartment buildings. I had a key to Noble's apartment but he eventually changed the lock because Enid and I abused his kindness. In the Bahamas we could abuse the bedroom because we paid for it for two weeks. We were ready for vulgarity and mischief on the soiled mattress slept on by other tourists.

    She bathed, dolled up, undressed like a call girl, and I liked her sophistication. I'd gone that route before so I knew different undressing styles. Off came my gift which was a scarf with the word *Fats,* bought from Alice, the store owner in the American Express Building in Lower Manhattan. There I saw President Gerald Ford and Frank Sinatra close up as they walked by. Sinatra's eyes were the bluest I'd seen. Fats unhooked the fake pearl worn on her wedding day and placed it carefully on the night table as if it were the real deal from Tiffany's.

    A fitted dress unzipped from behind left her body and fell to the floor. A slip rested on her see-through bra. The bra, minimized, held only half of her breasts. She eased off everything. She looked at me and turned away, but I glimpsed her hardened nipples. The cheeks of her bum in an undersized, flesh-colored panty, overflowed.

She bent forward as a carnival clown on stilts, pulled off her knee-high stockings; her booty at an acute angle faced me, the string of her napkin-sized panty collapsed. Her erotic posture was sinfully inviting. Yet my mind roamed.

My mind first roamed to my paramour in Brooklyn and to my youthful days in Fyzabad. But it stayed on my youth spent on The Bridge in Fyzabad. The Bridge was a log about eight yards long over a dam with alligators and about seventy five yards from my mother and stepfather's house. There I learned imaginative sex and my pubescent hairs grew when I listened to sex taught by older boys who learned from other boys a year or so older.

As a boy, most nights I went to bed and dreamed of the day that I would have sex with Miss Root. Alvin Thomas said her breasts were big as grapefruits, and her vagina was deep like a Vauxhall seat. Miss Root broke him in, and he didn't cry. My dream came true. But at my indoctrination I couldn't stand the pain from my foreskin, and I screamed, "Miss Root, Miss Root, it's hurting, it's hurting."

"Get off under me, you damn cry-cry baby."

I went home in pain and blood. My mother rushed me to San Fernando General Hospital to have me circumcised and never asked what had happened to me. But she knew I went by Miss Root. We lived at the bottom of the hill; Miss Root lived on the hill top; and my mother saw my ascent.

Why were all these distractions bugging me when Fats undressed?

The themes of the bigger boys on The Bridge echoed in my brain: "Take it from me, Hollis, when sexing your girl boast like hell, and boasting will give you confidence and make your dick get big and hard as a rock. And you must give your girl a pet name when you are doing rudeness with her. Uncle Dee said that."

"Boast about what?" someone had asked. I listened to the answer. I wish I could tell now who had asked that question but that was over 60 years ago.

"Boast about yourself and your family. Uncle Dee told me that you must say something to get your woman mad, and when a woman is mad in bed, it taste better. He said Old Spice on your body makes your girl croon, and giving her a pet name makes her feel special." That answer came from one of the bigger boys, an understudy to Uncle Dee, and all the boys from on top the hill and those in the gulley were students of Uncle Dee.

I had ingested that advice on sex behavior and my penis rose, but it fell limp when the discussion ended. As a boy I enjoyed both movements of my penis, especially when it moved up.

On my belated honeymoon I was a grown man and should have refrained from recycling childhood fables from The Bridge. But I didn't.

Enid rubbed on me and my mind went back to her naked body in the Bahamas.

I held her. I was ready to exhibit all my childhood and manhood fantasies in a ludicrous and playful fashion to engender love, and laughter, with sex. I was *cock sure* my lovemaking would dispel the argument we had on Paradise Island, the showcase of the Bahamas. She had caught me passing my phone number to a woman.

Cock sure is not surety, I learned. I don't ever use that word now.

"Fats, I like the color of this bedroom." I touched her tenderly.

"Why you waited so long to touch me there?"

My answer was a big lie.

"Why did you call me *Fats* when we first did it in Noble's house?"

I lied again, and she knew.

We laughed aloud.

"You know how I waited on this day to come." She giggled. Giggling was her sign of euphoria.

"You waited on the day to come or for the gristle?"

"Both."

There are lots of dumb Romeos in bed. I was the dumbest. I began my asinine boasting for my foreplay as if I were still eleven years old and was sitting on The Bridge: "Fats, let me tell you before I put it in." I stroked her pubic hairs. "My sister in England is a trained nurse, more qualified than any of your brothers and sisters."

From the look in her eyes and the sudden listlessness of her body, I knew I bombed with foot-in-mouth disease by invoking *The Bridge Sex Education Technique* taught by Uncle Dee: Getting a woman angry in bed makes her horny and her sexing is best.

Immediately, I remembered that only she

could berate her siblings, especially her brother, William "The Tank" Bain. He got the nickname on the soccer field. In midfield he had heard his sister's loud voice in dispute. He rushed out of his position as right back, tanked down her tormentor with fisticuffs, ran back to the soccer field, and defended his goalie from the opposing striker. The Tank's pugilism on the eastern corridor of Trinidad is still remembered by his peers.

Usually, my penis ruled my head, and I would have inserted, pronto, instead of giving a treatise were it another lover. That day in the Bahamas Uncle Dee's education caused a storm in the blue bedroom.

My "hard on" turned into soft dough. I was now thinking as an adult. But it was too late. The room was so silent that the rain sounded as a hurricane on the zinc roof. She pushed me away and spoke without calling my name.

"The Tank has a Ph.D. Vernon, a math scholar, graduated from UWI, and he was in the company of His Royal Highness the Duke of Edinburgh at the University of the West Indies. You have Vernon's picture with Prince Charles among your treasured souvenirs. And you show people Vernon's picture when you want to boast of leaving the corn fields and marrying up into the Bains family." She paused. "My sisters are highly-paid professionals. They are too dignified to be compared with *any of your ugly sisters*." She looked at me as if I were Judas. "Your little sister is a fake nurse in England cleaning English feces."

I cursed her to offset her hurt to me.

Her retorts continued, not a word obscene, but her description of me and my siblings hurt every organ in my body.

"One day your tongue will melt like Metro's ice in the sun!" I shouted.

"You ain't tired telling me that shit." She snatched her clothes off the floor, ran into the bathroom, slammed the door, and dry paint fell off of it.

"I should have listened to my mother. She warned me about marrying your type."

"Stop breathing through spaghetti, asshole. Your mother wanted you to marry the half-Indian woman. But she dumped your ass."

I jumped into my pajamas, no longer a loin cloth.

We traded salvoes of hurt on the night of

our so-called honeymoon. But I couldn't match her jousts.

Our two-week stay in the Bahamas was barely civil.

On the plane to New York, she sat in the fuselage. She exchanged seat with a passenger. Not even our clothes shared company in our luggage.

Time is a healer, for some. It was for us.

A Saturday night in January I had come home late from jazz in the Village Vanguard after I dropped my date home. I turned on the light.

"Surprise!"

Enid's friends were there to celebrate my fiftieth birthday. I had stopped introducing her to my friends because I never knew what day was full moon for her. Even at the book reading of my novel, *Grenada Ghost,* at Medgar Evers College she made some of my female friends uncomfortable.

She never kept a birthday party for me before because early in our marriage I told her that I'm antisocial and hated any get-together for me. The reason was: I was afraid of letting her know my friends. She toasted the affirmation of her undying love for me. "I'll always be there for you, Hollis, whatever the ebb and flow of the tides in our lives."

"I thank you, Fats." I was moved by her prose.

"Tell Fats that she'll be getting the best lovemaking tonight," Myrtle Stuart said. Myrtle was Enid's best friend, and the godmother of our daughter, Gail.

"Mind your business, Miss Parliament." Myrtle had worked as my typist when I was a Parliament reporter, and she had won the Miss Parliament Beauty Contest.

My fiftieth birthday turned out to be our b*elated-belated honeymoon*. We didn't disappoint each other's desires. It was a great night in bed.

"Where you learned to spike so hard, Fats?"

"When you forced me to look at Monday night football, I saw what those guys did with the ball after a touch down. You liked it?"

"Yes."

"That was my gift."

We laughed as new lovers. We had sex after every meal. Our love flowed swiftly and smoothly. We were humming birds pollinating the hibiscus flowers in the early tropical morn while dew is forming on the green leaves. Then the sun came out. We looked at each other and jumped on the bed again.

The next day, as if performing in an official capacity, as if my birthday were something of the distant past, she became cerebral.

"I saw how you were looking at the woman who came with Myrtle. I didn't drink Jim Jones's kool aid in Guyana, so I'm not stupid!"

"I'm stupid about you only, Fats."

"I don't believe you."

"I do."

"You have a lot to prove, nighttime Romeo – not in bed, but in truthfulness."

3

Life's journey is a testament that a successful marriage is not lightly achieved. Our marriage is proof.

There was a truce in our conflict. Call it deceitful *détente.* The truth blacksmith hammered our tongues, somewhat. Time bleached the greater part of our hubris. And praises for each other's kindness and "strength perspective" replaced our brickbats of toxic answers to simple questions. We stopped turning our backs to each other at bedtime. We slept in each other's arms, even after earlier fights. Some nights I wished she wasn't in my arms because I felt guilty of my infidelity.

But "something was wrong" at **519.** If anybody had a clue of what was wrong, Enid did. But she never divulged it. And I lived in denial of all those clues. She couldn't find her things: her treasury—her purse; her freehold property—her car keys; her leasehold property—her house keys. She didn't call the tenants in her commercial building on the last day of the month to inform, "You'll definitely see me tomorrow for my rent." These were clues of memory loss that I should have seized on. I didn't because she still disciplined her children. To prevent Taariq, our oldest son, from hanging out in Nostrand Park, a drug hole at that time, she sent our children to a Seventh Day Adventist Church. "Taariq, you have to come to my church on Sunday but you need God on Saturday, too." Beresford Moore, the assistant pastor, and the only mechanic she let under her Buick, drove her home but her house keys were not in her purse. He then drove her to the Seventh Day Adventist Church on Kingston Avenue.

"Call my children for me! I want to borrow their keys." It was a rainy Saturday.

"Pastor Crooks, I have not seen your children for sometime now," Austin Tuitt, pastor in training, said. "I thought you took them away from this church."

Our children were at every hamburger joint for those missed Sabbath days. They spent their church offering on hamburgers and hot dogs. Judy was the ringleader of the hamburger gang. When

I picked up the strap to bluff punishment for cutting Sabbath school, Judy cried out, "Daddy, don't beat me. I'm getting blind."

Judy's faked blindness became our blind joke. But Enid warned, "Hollis, if ever you let my child get blind you'd have to live on the street." She felt only she had the authority to punish our children.

I began to pay attention to all of Enid's moves. I never snooped on her before. To me, watching someone is degrading one's self. I noticed she had several car keys, and she boasted about everything as if that gave her confidence in herself.

"How much are you making on your job? Why not come and work at Con Edison with me?"

As a customer service representative at Consolidated Edison, she calculated the price of electric consumption by customers. She had helped another employee who forgot her math. That employee has since died from Alzheimer's disease. The computer was introduced, and her aptitude for grasping the new technique was nil. It baffled me when she spoke with sadness of her inability to learn the new system. She had told me when students were puzzled over stocks and shares in high school, the teacher sent her to the blackboard to teach the class.

I'd gone to take her to lunch. I saw that she alternated her movements behind the backs of Sherlene Blake and Fakita Moore. She waited for their assistance to do her job. Her bills piled up on the table, not opened. Her checkbooks, not sequentially numbered, were on the table, too.

She insisted that I should cook. "Let me handle my business." There was no need to tell me that because she always handled her business, and I was the permanent cook and the parent who went to parent-teacher meetings. The carpenter came and fixed the front door. "That's not the way my father fixed a door. You didn't bevel here; you didn't sandpaper here." She refused to pay him, but I did.

I was still on-and-off as the church pianist. "I think people are coming to church to hear Pastor Crooks sing rather than to hear her preach," her assistant pastor said within earshot. He probably knew I was disgusted with her *new kind of gospel*, as he was, that mostly spoke of her pranks in youth. When we came home, she asked, "How I did today?" My answer was, "Your singing was great." I mentioned nothing about her rambling gospel that said nothing about the bible.

"You know who taught me to sing every part to a hymn?"

"You told me your father did."

He was her unending thesis. Her large nostrils, like his, quivered when she spoke. "Father used to put Silvie, Vernon, Willy, Pearl, Versil, and me to sing a hymn, and he went outside and listened to the part each of us sang. Then he came inside and said, 'Enid you were the best.' Then he said, 'Some of those ministers and priests who have you all singing hymns are scamps and fornicators. I work for them on their church buildings, and I see what they do.'" She laughed as if her father were there and enjoyed that moment with her.

She never sought out cousins or phoned them. She called them "pumpkin-vine" family. But somehow she was always phoning Emris Bain, her father's niece.

Emris phoned one day, and I answered.

"Hollis, is Enid home?"

"No." She was glad to hear that news.

"Enid told me that she's getting the same *thing* Father died from. Father suffered with that *thing* for so long. He used to walk away, and we had to go and search for him. Sometimes he went many miles away, and because he was a known building contractor many of the people he built houses for brought him home to Mom. If Enid knows I told you that she's getting Father's disease she'd *kill me dead.*" She repeated, "*She'll kill me dead.*"

Trinidad and Tobago people, nicknamed "Trinis," speak in the vernacular for speed talking, flavoring the superlative, and making the "positive," in the degree of comparison, become the superlative: *Good* takes the place of *best*. Overworking the obvious is also a *Trini thing*. Here's an example of Dora telling Jane about a dispute she had with Sarah: "Jane girl, I cussed Sarah *good.*" *Good* meant that Dora had cursed Sarah to her utmost satisfaction. *Better* or *best* would not have driven home the impact of Dora's dirty tongue.

I, a born Trini, now an American by naturalization, also overworked the obvious. "Fats *would really kill me dead too* if she knew that I was talking about Alzheimer's with you. I told someone she has early Alzheimer's and she went berserk."

Emris hung up in fear of her cousin's shadow who, at that time, could have been miles away looking for her Buick not knowing where she had parked it. Not knowing where she had parked her Buick became common place in the middle stage of her Alzheimer's.

We planned another lunch date. I stayed a distance away and mingled with customers who waited to be called by customer service representatives. The sadness on my wife's face was so pronounced when she waited for help from Sherlene or Fakita before she left for lunch. Each representative had a quota to fill.

At the Jamaican restaurant, I asked, "Is anything wrong, Fats? I saw you standing behind Sherlene and Fakita instead of attending to the customers."

"Why are you staying so long to order the food?" She changed the subject.

I could no longer broach the subject I had in mind but came to the conclusion that something was wrong with her; she knew what was wrong and kept it as a secret.

In 1992, Sullivan & Cromwell offered a package of early retirement to employees 50 years and over. I was 58 and welcomed the package. The day I signed the resignation document was the first day in my life in the Wall Street district that I came home immediately after work. I didn't go gallivanting, girl watching, or head for midtown peepholes. I had to share my joy with Fats. It was as if coming events were casting their shadows: that I needed to stop working to take care of my wife.

Enid resigned at age 62. I thanked Sherlene Blake and Fakita Moore at Enid's party. A year later Fakita died. At Fakita's funeral, Enid cried like a baby. When she retired I believed staying at home and not seeing the traffic on her job, even though she couldn't do her job, slowed her ability to do simple duties.

She shocked me at the dinner table one morning. "Help me with these." She pushed her checkbooks and bills for me. For over an hour she had shuffled everything on the table and did not know what to do with the papers in front of her. I wept inside. I was angry that she was losing the fight and no longer pretended that she was in control.

* * * * *

No matter what our conversation, Father became the *non sequitur.* He was a short man, five-foot-one, without an ounce of fat, and strong as an ox. He was a teetotaler. His large nostrils made him look shorter. His ears were seen the same time his bald-plated head was. His smarts were visible on the plate of his head. He spoke and laughed at the same time, and his laughter complemented his speech, *vice versa.* His shoe soles were twisted by the emphasis on them. He rallied his workers to hurry up with the job because he believed the construction of a building should take a certain amount of time, and no more. I watched his workmanship when he built our house in Trinidad. He doodled over the building plan with the pencil taken from behind his ears. "Enid girl, come look at your house plan." Enid looked at it. "You want to change anything in the plan, girl?" Whatever she wanted changed, he did it.

He was a kind man. At times, he paid his workmen more than himself. His kindness brought heated arguments with his wife. He always handed her his pay envelope and addressed her at the same time. "Otterly, my workers have little children, and all our children are big and employed, so don't question me about the money in that envelope."

Otterly had the last word.

Enid told us for the umpteenth time the Enos-Otterly upheavals over the sharing of a pack of ground nuts and how her father needed the Price Waterman Accounting firm to elicit fairness in the distribution of grains in a 4-ounce pack. She spoke as if her parents were in Kodak Theatre, live in performance, before they accepted their Oscars.

"Nos boy, take this." Otterly never pronounced the *E*. "But, Otterly, this is only two grains from that big pack of nuts in your lap."

"I bought it. Here's more, Nos."

"This is only one grain more. I gave you my full pay in the envelope. I never burst my envelope."

"But this is *my* nuts. I bought it, and I have the right to share it how I want to." Give me some more."

"Nos, ask your workers to buy a pack of nuts for you next payday."

Enid laughed, and stopped, and finished

her mother's reply. "Nos, you are the boss, and you gave your workers more pay than youself, so ask them to buy a pack of nuts for you when you pay them next week." She shifted from memory to memory of her past in Trinidad and Tobago.

"Father took me to every new construction site. He let me work out the board foot for each room. He checked to see if my math were correct. He showed me all the angles in the room and how he had cut those angles in wood, and how he bent steel. He let me mix cement, and I became a pro at it."

Mom got her admiration from Enid, but it never lasted for thirty seconds. She hated Mom's circumspectness in things that related to her boyfriend, Horace Gordon: "Enid, I'm always dressing you up like a doll, getting Silvie, the best seamstress in Tunapuna, to put appliqués in your clothes, and you have *that naked* boy coming to my house every time in the same half-dirty-half-clean clothes to pick you up." She mimicked Mom. "Father was more understanding. He never showed Horace a bad face, even though he preferred...." She forgot the name of her other boyfriend. "Father always gave me pocket money.

He said when a boy gives any girl money he would want the girl to pay him with her body."

Her next topic was about her idol. "Gamma was preaching and Brother Dennis was humming a hymn. Gamma had warned him *never* hum hymns when she was preaching. Brother Dennis forgot. Gamma came off the pulpit, butted him to the ground, and nobody helped him up because he was warned."

Somehow I felt she was up-ticking her image. "That isn't true, Fats!"

"That is true! I lived with Gamma until I was 11 years old. Her church was in her backyard. And I was always there in church with Gamma. I like the way she preached, and probably that's why I like to preach."

"You lived with Gamma all those years and adopted her Spiritual Baptist religion. You came to the United States and joined a similar church. People called you Mother Crooks because you had a high position in their spiritual hierarchy. You were also the secretary of that church. How come you left that faith, went to Logos Bible College, a Pentecostal institution, and after graduation instead of going back to your Spiritual Baptist Church, you opened a non-denominational church and worshipped in a different way from Spiritual Baptists?"

She didn't understand the question. I, too, got lost in the question. I felt like those interviewers on TV who love to purposely corner their guests to show that they are more learned on the subject than their guests and ask long, confusing questions. But I had asked her that exact question when she graduated from Logos, and she "ate up the question like cooked food."

Her answer then was a treatise that made me feel proud. She quoted scripture and verse to show my ignorance of the Bible. She was the batsman who knew what kind of ball I would pitch and waited on my delivery to hit me out of the park. "Hollis, I could understand why Gamma, an uneducated cane farmer, behaved as she did, and still people like Brother Dennis came to her church to get butted down. But when I joined the Spiritual Baptist in this country, and I knew the pastor, the head of that Spiritual Baptist Church, couldn't read...."

"How you found out he didn't know Peter from Paul in the Bible?"

"Because I had to tell him...When I was under his spell and saw that he had such a hold on all those people and *me*, I looked at myself as if I were Brother Dennis and waited on him to butt me. Don't you think so?"

"Sure." I was remembering the past and the way she reasoned.

"Do you remember what members said when I was the secretary of that Spiritual Baptist Church and gave a Vote of Thanks and thanked members for their *invaluable service*?"

"I was there. I remember the ruckus. They misinterpreted the meaning of *invaluable service*. They rebuked you. 'You, Enid Crooks, Miss Flatbush, is telling us that *our service to this church has no value*! Who you think you are?'"

"If I'd stayed in that congregation I would have been just like you forever in John Jules's atheist class. You took in all that junk from Jules about there's no God. Probably, Jules, too, couldn't read. Don't tell me about your favorite book, Thomas Paine's *Age of Reason*, that Jules gave you as a present. Tell me about the *Bible*, fool. My wish for you is that you'll read the Bible."

She lectured me then. And I loved it. That was "my Fats turned Pastor Crooks, the preacher." Every man should love his wife a little more when she boasts about herself as a confident woman.

I adore a confident woman. I wouldn't say I love them with my eyes closed.

This time my question was not understood. Her escape was her favorite subject—Father, Father, Father.

Every night she ransacked her drawers. Yet I lived in denial that Alzheimer's had begun to rule her life because most nights I could not find an old tie to band my aching waist. "What are you looking for, Fats?"

"That's not your business!"

She stopped preparing her sermons.

One night she had church in her bedroom and read *Isaiah 1-18: Come now, and let us reason together, saith the Lord: though your sins be as scarlet, they shall be as white as snow; though they be red like crimson, they shall be as wool.*

We prayed, and she poured out her heart and begged God to fill her church with members. I prayed just as loud as she, but I said nothing about my trysts lest she ended Isaiah's, abruptly.

Taariq refused to pray. She had encouraged him to leave her church and join a youth-oriented church where he became an altar boy. His new minister, an erudite male specimen, had come to our home, uninvited, and rushed to our basement

where Taariq played his guitar. The minister rushed back upstairs. Enid rushed downstairs. "Why your minister left so quickly?" "He wanted to play up with me. And he'd never get that from me."
"What!" Her descriptions of that man of God could not be written, only one word in *Trini* parlance I dare write. "You'd be coming back to my church where no stinking rapist can ask you for *mandom*."
She dumped Taariq's church vestment in the garbage and spat on them.

*   *   *   *

She, Judy, and I sat around the table. We discussed the deterioration of the block. It was somewhat of an anomaly that Enid did not dominate the conversation. Instead, she focused on TV commercials. Since I had taken on the new role of watching all her moves, I noticed she was only interested in commercials that advertised brain food. She took a mental note of brain commercials. While those commercials invaded the air space, she took a pill. I dare not ask what she swallowed.

Judy said, "Daddy, I hate to come here and look for you and my mother. There are too many stray cats running around. How does mammy get out? You know she hates cats with a passion."

"When a boy, I had a bad experience with cats. My mother's cat had new-born babies in the clothes basket, and a tomcat killed every male. I had to bury the dead cats."

Enid shouted without warning. "Judy, take me to the hospital. My tongue is getting hot."

In Kings County Hospital Emergency, the doctor told Judy she could accompany her mother inside. Enid told him that she's a big woman and didn't want any company. After she was attended to and discharged, Judy asked, "Mammy, why was your tongue hot? What happened?"

"The doctor said I had too much garlic in my system."

"Mammy, did you tell the doctor it could be from an overdose of all those imported remedies that you are taking and have hidden away?"

"I birthed you. You didn't make me, so you can't tell me what to do."

Judy slipped away from her, called me, and told me her mother's diagnosis.

I became a diligent detective and searched **519** thoroughly. In high closets where I'd never gone before, I found boxes of imported or ordered stuff with only the post office labels. The senders' names and addresses were ripped off. On a box, with Enid's handwriting, barely visible, were the letters *FTB*. Another box, with countless pills, unraveled the code: *For The Brain.*

Her for-the-brain remedies were not authorized by the Food and Drug Administration. But I dare not dump them without her permission. So I adopted a new detective style: As an infomercial came on about *brain food*, I said, "Poison!"

She listened to me when I berated her remedies. But I also knew my wife's temperament. I got burned so many times in the past for my transgressions: for doing or saying things about which she had opposing views. Once upon a time the controversy of social justice never swayed her one way or the other. She was always the construct of her being. "Only I should make laws for my body."

One day during her agreeable mood, I coaxed her to follow me to our internist. She seemed eager to go, and I seized the opportunity. So unlike when I had asked her to go to a doctor and she had blurted, "You are older than me! Why don't you go yourself?" She was so riled by my suggestion that she preached a gospel on *Old Men who think they are still young.* She likened that old man, me, with Matthew 7:4: Some husbands "pull out the mote from their wives' eyes; but if they had pulled out the beam from their *own* eyes first, they would have seen the mote in their wives' eye better."

On the advice of internist Dr. Lalasa Valasareddi, Dr. Ramaswami Sundar became Enid's neurologist. He confirmed my suspicion of her cognitive symptoms that haunted me in Mozambique. In Mozambique, President Chissano had offered her the opportunity to preach at any church of her choice. She turned down his offer twice. When Pastor Crooks trusted her cognitive ability, she would have snatched that opportunity to come back and boast to members of her church: *I preached in Mozambique, and the President was there. God had promised me that He will let me preach in Africa.* Her refusal to preach on the African Continent, a dream she had hoped come true since her graduation from Logos, confirmed my suspicion that she lost that "wave of self-esteem" and self confidence that was her trademark. I knew from research that soon she wouldn't be able to "self-advocate."

Somehow though, she knew her limit. She didn't want her sermon to be said without authority. She didn't want her Mozambican congregation to find her lukewarm. In lucidity, she said, "I will never preach a lukewarm gospel. I will be fiery whenever I preach God's Word." She knew her fire was outing, or out. I wish I knew what made her think so.

Dr. Sundar examined her in private. In my presence, he asked her to repeat the five words he had told her to memorize. (I later learned from Dr. Howard Crystal, her present neurologist, that term is called "immediate recall.") She could not remember any of the words. He pointed at the wall clock and asked the time. She didn't know it. "Who am I, and what do I do?" She didn't know. "Where are you now?" She didn't know. "What date is it?" She didn't know. "Who's the President of the United States? What's your address?" She looked at me for the answers.

He left me in his office. He walked her to his waiting room and seated her there under the watchful eye of his secretary. In his absence, I looked out the window and saw Brooklyn's blue skies. I once thought Jesus Christ lived in that blue sky. I was taught that in Sunday school. My next thought was Jesus Christ would let Dr. Sundar give me good news about my wife's health. My mind raced, and I then looked at the picture of a Hindu image on the wall, with the *sindoor*, which is the bright red dot in the center of the image's forehead. The image has extra hands, and I wondered if that image were the doctor's god who advised him on medicine.

Dr. Sundar's footsteps brought me back to the moment. He closed his door noisily and gained my attention. He sat and studied Enid's files. I interrupted him, and said, verbatim, a psychotherapist's findings that I'd memorized: "Doctor, my wife doesn't know her current behavior and the consequences to her."

"Your wife has Alzheimer's. The receptionist will give you an appointment for the next visit."

I could see he wished he had given me better news.

My thoughts deepened. *Fats will die from Alzheimer's like her father.*

Next morning I waited for the Sanitation truck. I held three boxes of *FTB*'s. The sanitation man stretched for them, but I dumped the for-the-brain remedies myself and heard them crushed in the packer.

Enid's illness drew me close to her, close like my skin on my body. Her wounded body became my blanket of thought. It told me that I should know whenever she is hungry. I should know when she is wet, hurt, in need of another pillow, in need of my love. And because of this miscellany of thoughts that she was unable to express, my "lull hour" was no longer mine. It was hers.

Her good-health levees broke. Her immunity, pomp, and pride are now shattered. Her AD wagons holes of pain in me. Only her eyes speak. I am her mental dictionary and interpreter. Once I was irked when she washed both hands and dried each joint on her fingers, clockwise, and counterclockwise, up and down. God knew then that I had sinned in thought when I was overburdened with onerous duties. But I studied her new habits because it was my way of learning how to cope with early, middle, and the late stages of Alzheimer's.

"Leave me alone. You're not Mom," she said in the early stage. Her mother's love and their conflict in childhood were like an elegy. When she spoke, I thought of my mother's life: *Why God made mammy so poor? Why she had to go in the fields every day to make a living for her children? Why she kept me from school so many days to go in the fields with her?*

Those "whys" were concrete stanchions of self-pity that I had logged around, and Enid offloaded them with humor and *her* philosophy when she was lucid. "Hollis, they were the foundation of your strength, and because of your strength I have learned a lot even when I boasted about myself. Your children have told me that they admire your strength, but they are uncomfortable when expressing their love for you. You've got to loosen up, Hollis. They are afraid to hug you. You told me that you have never seen your father or stepfather hug your mother. That was then. We live in a now world. You are good at making jokes. Make a joke and when they laugh, hug them and laugh louder. Try that."

"I tried that on Trish."

"Daddy, why are you so stiff whenever I hug you?" she said.

4

Before my stepfather moved in with my mother and her three children—he eventually married her—we lived in dire hardship, and there was dearth, dearth, everywhere. Mammy waited on her crops to be harvested to get money for our upkeep. Yet she refused employment, for her children's sake, for the best paying job for black women in the oilfields. Their pay was $0.03 an hour. Women toted trays of mud on their heads and cleared locations for the erection of platforms and derricks for drilling for oil. Men were the diggers. Women were the haulers who did the work of tractors in dangerous places.

I was glad mammy, named Leoni Crooks, never took that job. Mud-toting women in Fyzabad oilfields, especially in TLL, were nicknamed "Tattoo Women." The middle class people used the nickname in a degrading way. Tattoo was, and probably still is, the villagers' name for an agouti which is an edible rodent whose habitat is a hole. The rodent enters into one hole and digs another hole in the opposite direction to make its escape from hunters.

Had mammy taken that bonanza of a job, she envisioned my brother, Paul, and I would have been nicknamed "Tattoo Hollis...Tattoo Paul" throughout our school life. She knew Paul would have fought his way out. But she knew that I was a coward and had a penchant for revenge. For sure, schoolmates who continued to call me "Tattoo Hollis" would have found cattle dung in their lunch pails kept in the cloak room. Mammy stored an abundance of dried cattle dung because our house was built with dried dung, mud, sticks, and grass. Water was the glue for those materials to repair our house.

I was prevented from writing the high school entrance examination because of poor school attendance. Having good attendance was a strict rule of the Trinidad and Tobago Board of Education. Mammy cleared the forest and cultivated quick crops. Most times TLL oil wells overflowed, and the rain and oil spillage wrecked her produce. TLL never compensated her because she was a squatter. She had to start all over again, penniless. I knew she was penniless because she had cursed Mrs. Jules, the atheist's wife; Magistrate Cazabon charged her a shilling (twenty four cents); and someone paid the fine. I suspected it was my absentee father.

Enid romanticized her childhood. She spoke of her popularity in high school. "I was a star. I sang on *Radio Trinidad* more than once. My music teacher, Undine Giuseppi, loved my voice in her choir."

When she spoke of her father's building contracting job and her mother's sizable freehold properties, I thought of my mother's hands that rooted crops from the soil.

"You always speak about your mother. What your father did?"

"I didn't grow up with him, and he hadn't much to give, but I loved him."

"I'm talking about business. You're talking about love. Each has its place. I'm tired of telling you that."

During our nightly conversations when she probed my father's past, my thoughts strayed to the years when he left my mother with three children. I remembered him happy as a lark when he worked temporarily as a barman in TLL and played the piano for the staff members. He had come to my mother's gap and handed me three single dollars for three children. The bills were blue. "Take this money for Loney." He walked away, and I ran inside. "Mammy, daddy gave us plenty money."

Months had passed before we saw him again. This time he hadn't money for Paul, Gloria, and me. He wasn't a tailor, but he altered his clothes to fit Paul and me, and brought a dinner mint for Gloria. Mammy's tongue was poison when he brought no money. Still he came to see his children. Paul never cared for him. He purposely went down the gully and played with the pigs. But I grieved when he left. He made his *presence* his business; and, to me, his *presence* was money, victual, and priceless love. His sporadic *presence* was like gold because I was not yet used to seeing my stepfather as the man in the house even though my stepfather was a very nice man. I realized how nice he was when I became a parent and looked back into the past. My children could say I am a womanizer but they can also say I am a provider.

Under the shady hackberry in our backyard my thoughts were always in motion. I thought of the way my father in his mid-forties put down his guitar and played his saxophone. He sight read music effortlessly, and he knew what piece he'd play on his saxophone when a light-skinned woman passed by. I didn't know the song, but I remembered that song had long notes because he blew those notes until that "high brown woman" got out of sight. On his 90th birthday, he handed me his first letter of employment in the oilfield. I barely made out *194*....It was parchment paper. That letter was his silent testimony to let me know that "money was scarce but he always loved his children."

I loved my mother, stepfather, and godmother dearly. They were responsible for my upbringing. But even though my father was not around, I'd loved him most. His name was Leonard Alister Brathwaite.

My mother tried to put reality into my life when I was a little boy. "Tiger can't get a long-term job to mind his three children because he's lazy. He's only looking for jobs where he doesn't have to sweat." Reality meant nothing to me compared to my love for him.

A happy day came again when my father brought three dollars for his three children's upkeep and my mother's dimple deepened with a smile. "Tiger, you want a tumbler of water?" She invited him inside.

"Loney, since I moved to Tobago, I don't drink Trinidad water again. Trinidad water's not sweet." He pulled out a bottle of Tobago rain water from his bag and quenched his thirst.

I visited him in Tobago, and he took me for a ride on his motorcycle. I was 45. He was 69. I came off the back of his motorcycle and said, without warning, "Why you left us, daddy, and married Miss Ruth? Is it because mammy is black and Miss Ruth has a light complexion?" I relieved a burden that I had carried around all my life.

"It's not that." He knew I didn't believe him but he continued. "It is because Loney cursed too much for nothing." He stuttered. "Ruthie never cursed, and she does everything for me... anything." He called his wife Ruthie. She called him Ali.

I spent two weeks with him and Ruthie. Her service to my father bordered on serfdom.

"Ali, are you ready for your breakfast?"

"No, Ruthie."

Twenty seconds later. "Ruthie, I'm ready. Bring it downstairs."

Fifteen seconds later. "Ruthie, come

downstairs and bring some sugar for me." She brought the sugar and went back upstairs. He called out: "Ruthie, not granulated sugar." She came back downstairs with brown sugar, sweetened his tea, and tasted it. "See if it's all right, Ali." He tasted it. "It's good now, Ruthie. Thank you." She went back upstairs.

"Boy, see what I was talking about? No matter how many times I called Ruthie, she came without a frown. Not your mother. She'd curse me from beginning to end."

His house rested on the turn of the steep road in Whim village. It was destroyed by hurricane Flora, and he rebuilt it without help. We sat in the gallery and Julie mangoes dropped incessantly. But our eyes were on passersby.

"Boy, look at that nice, brown-skinned baby that girl has in her hand."

I blasted off like a rocket. "You still talk that color-prejudice shit!"

Ruthie rushed into the gallery. "Don't bother with Ali. I don't know when he'd end that stupid talk." She picked up his dirty dishes and asked him what else he needed.

I didn't know that my mind had gone that deep into the past when Fats and I sat under the hackberry that began to shed yellow leaves. "What are you thinking of now, Hollis?" Enid's knew when my mind roamed. She could tell when my mind was on a woman, or on an event.

"Fats, I'm thinking of what I said at Tiger's funeral: 'Daddy, you taught your children how to cope with nothing and live with hope. We need nothing, but air. To love, we need not say *I love you*, but show it in our action. In grief, kind words are better than pennies.'" Tiger was like an Ethiopian motherboard. He knew everything about his parents, their parents' parents, and their occupations. At age 89, he dictated four generations of his family tree. He wanted me to be the new *griot* of his clan. He was so proud of me. "Do I have to smell my grandbabies?" I had asked him. He smiled, and I saw how handsome he still was. I loved him so much.

Fats rested her hand on my shoulder and said, "It's time to stop thinking and eat." I became emotional as yellow leaves fell from the hackberry into my plate.

We were born in 1934, but our war years were seen through different prisms. Enid was never in the ration lines. I can't remember if she had told me whether her brothers, Vernon and Willy, were in those ration lines, but she said Mom had a contact to get staple food in a place called Bejucal. When I told her of my disguises and changed voices to look differently and sound differently every time to get ration food—rice, bread, sugar, flour--from the Chinese and Portuguese shopkeepers in Fyzabad—she made funny faces. Her comedy followed. "Boy, you were really poor. You had jigger, too? Had I known you then, I would not have spoken to you."

"But, mammy, you were poor, too," Judy said. "In your time everybody was poor."

"Not that kind of poor to change my voice to get food. I changed my voice range when I was singing on *Radio Trinidad*." She threw herself on the floor and laughed aloud.

I loved when Fats teased me. But I preferred when she boasted to our children and dramatized our juxtaposed upbringing: me the pauper; she the princess. In her prime there was laughter galore at **519**. She made our different upbringing golden and more golden, no matter how I looked at it. She had all the spices of love for today and tomorrow. And her spices were always freshly ground.

But "there was a fly in the ointment" I couldn't see.

Lloyd Hollis Crooks

5

With impaired memory, her tenants ganged up on her and never paid their rent for many months.

I became the landlord, without experience. Sometimes the tenants didn't open their doors when I knocked. Sometimes they did. Why I tasked myself this job... It should be given to a real estate agent, I thought. Then I knock.

"I'll only pay your wife," Mondeez said. That's not her real name, but that's what she said.

"I have the power of attorney to collect my wife's rent, and I will give you a receipt for whatever money you pay me," I reasoned.

"I only deal with Mrs. Crooks!"

"She has Alzheimer's. She can no longer read, write, nor count."

"She is who I will deal with!"

Mondeez, and the other tenants, never paid rent when they realized Enid's illness made her unable to keep books. Mondeez showed me her bookkeeping and said, "This place has rats, so we won't pay you."

The exterminator came. Then I asked for the rent. It was not paid.

The City called me to turn on the tenants' heat. And I did. But the tenants still refused to pay their rent.

On those occasions Enid's advice came to mind. "Hollis, if ever you become in charge of my building, and I hope you *never* will. But should you, you should cross the street if you see a male dog or a bitch, with or without teeth."

"Why?" I had never heard that expression and didn't know its meaning. Probably that was one of Gamma's philosophies. She applied most of them.

"Because the male dog and the bitch are capable of giving you rabies."

"What if I didn't cross the street?" Still I hadn't an idea of what would be her answer.

"Be prepared to fight with those dogs and bitches to the end, until you win. You are such a coward and have no sense of business. All you do is cook. You still cannot play the piano after all these years. Your children, and so-called friends, twist you around their fingers. Just imagine, 8-year-old Trish, told you that she'd drop out of school and join a gang unless you increase her allowance. You took her bait and increased her allowance. Had that fresh-mouth Trish given me that ultimatum, she would have been a grandmother and still waiting for that increase."

I took Mondeez to court to be evicted from the apartment. The judge ruled in my favor after many months of deliberations and postponements. The Marshall put an eviction notice on Mondeez's door, and she ripped it off.

She took the judge's decision to a higher court.

I was stressed with landlord's problems and wasn't prepared to wait six months or more to win in court. Heating bills were high. Taxes were high. Maintenance of the building was costly. One tenant left without paying rental arrears but left her boyfriend in the apartment. He was an unauthorized tenant who knew his rights better than City Hall knew theirs.

How Enid handled these tenants crossed my mind every hour. I sold the building. I also caved in to the buyer's bargaining of a decrease in the sale price of $5000 for each tenant in the building at the date of sale. Mondeez was the only tenant when the building was sold. The other tenants did their damage to their apartments and left. The building was sold on September 5, 2002.

If Enid were lucid, she would have fought until she won in the higher court. She would *not* have sold her building for she believed in owning real estate. Her strength lay with her conviction. I was never able to step into her business shoe. But in sickness, I did. Many nights when I could not lift her out of the loveseat and put her in her wheelchair and wheel her to our bedroom and then lift her in bed, I slept on the loveseat with her wheelchair next to me. In the morning when I was rejuvenated after the help of *Ambien*, I went again to my loving duty with strength like Samson's.

The sale of her commercial property let me fleetingly see what a six-figure income was like, but that money was completely gone when I paid our debts: capital gains taxes, interest on taxes owed to IRS and the State, mortgage owed for **519**, credit cards, caregiving services, incidentals, hospitals, Attorney General's bill for money owed to Brooklyn Downstate Hospital, co-payments, ambulances, and doctors. Two of Enid's doctors always asked me, "Have you thought of putting your wife in a home?"

"No, Doctor. No, Doctor."

Dr. Avidah Rudberg's favorite line was, "You are a good man." His efficient nurse, Inessa Kunina, said in Russian, and she interpreted it in English, "God will bless you, Mr. Crooks, as I'm sure He blessed my uncle who took care of his wife, too." She drew my wife's blood, and looked at her pitifully, then to me.

My childhood experiences prepared me for caregiving. In the same way I had loved and cared for my mother, I now have that deep love for my wife. Never had I thought I would be paralleling both women's love, and gratitude. At ten years old I'd cooked a surprise dinner for my mother when she came from tending her crops many miles away. When she saw the table laid, she smiled. I can still hear the echo of her voice when she called me by my nickname—"Thank you, Blackboy," after she ate my undercooked meal, contentedly. Mammy's thankfulness to me for appeasing her hunger is on even keel with Enid's wordless thankfulness to me now seen in her eyes.

Her "loss of mutuality" and "loss of communication" were illustrated with her touch. She always put her hand on my forehead when I did her hygiene. I always thought she rested her hand on me to gain her balance, but her touch was a language that predated words. I eventually realized it was her pastor's touch of blessing. She touched my forehead the way she touched babies when she baptized them in a make-shift font in her church and bestowed her blessing on each baby. Trish and Khafra's baptisms never left my mind because of the way she prayed to God for their success in life. She probably, silently, prayed to God for me, too.

Some thoughts are nourishing when I compare her present and past states; others eke out every bit of hope in my imagination for her improvement. Enid believed in her hey-day that *faith* is the answer for swimmers and non-swimmers in the deep ocean who swam ashore. I believed *fate* is your fate, period. She called me godless because I said, "Jesus speaks of *faith*, and I believe in *fate*." One belief we had in common was we would fight out our marriage problems, without physical blows, and without a middleman as counselor. It wasn't easy.

I am now the businessman and risk taker, a job I never dreamed of. I think as the soldier in the foxhole for our sanity and survival: The soldier raises his helmet with a bayonet, and the sniper's bullet glides off the helmet. The soldier's buddy stays down. Both live to fight another day. Enid is my buddy. She's protected by my love which is my weapon. The sniper is Alzheimer's— a brute disguised in many clothing.

If I were the one with Alzheimer's disease, she would have pushed my wheelchair through the narrow doors of **519** for a short time only. Our house was never built to accommodate people with disability—the wheelchair cannot go into the bathroom, and I constantly damage the walls when I move it from one room to another. Without a doubt, Enid would have called in a carpenter and remodeled the bathroom. And with each stroke of the carpenter's hammer, she would have thought of Father. When she was healthy, every time I left on vacation, she renovated **519**. Her reason was, "I waited till you left because you would have objected." I always replied, "Fats, I never knew I had the power to prevent you from doing anything?" She'd smile that loving smile. "Okay."

On the road of time, a part of life was not seen until we made the bend. Once upon a time Enid's creative ability would have forecast that the roof would soon need covering before water trickled through the sheet rock. She would have known her insurance would be lowered because of her safe-driving record.

"Fats, what makes you a safe driver? You make a U-turn on a pin to get a parking spot?"

"Can you drive?"

"No."

"Then shut up."

She was emancipated from everything, except religion. A Jehovah's Witness rang our bell. She called them Bible Students. "That's what Mom and Father called them when I was growing up, and that is what I will call them. Aren't they the same people doing the same kind of gospel?"

"Yes, Fats." I let the woman in.

"Do you vote, Bible Student? I voted for George Pataki, the Republican, to be Governor; my husband voted for the loser, a Democrat. My pastor advised me on voting. Who advised you *not* to vote?" Enid looked at the Bible Student the way she looked at her children when they were lying about their absence from school.

The woman got pale. "Can I give you a copy of our *Watchtower* and *Awake*?"

"I don't read cult books."

Jehovah Witnesses knew **519** from a

distance. They skipped our house until one day a new Bible Student, scouting the neighborhood, rang our bell.

"Go and answer the bell. I'm sure it is those Bible Students coming to push their books in your face and lecture you. They don't listen to other people's gospel. Why do you read their books?"

"I read other religions'. Why should I not read theirs?"

"Invite them in." Shocked, I looked at her. "I say invite them in."

I knew that was a double anomaly: She wanted a fight; or her memory was getting worse. I met the woman at the door. She was dressed nicely, briefcase in one hand, books in another. I took two books, and handed her two dollars. "Sorry, Miss, I can't listen to you today." I closed the door softly.

If Enid's behavior is my guide and compass as to what to expect, I can now say Alzheimer's disease makes foes become friends....Puts the master at the mercy of the servant...And reminds us of the golden rule. The effect of Alzheimer's is powerful. It keeps me in the trenches, forever protecting my wife.

6

The disease began owning Enid's life. My infidelity was destroying it more. Pastoring Divine Truth Assembly was giving her solace, but her congregation was diminishing as fast as her memory.

Like a brute I maintained my philandering ways.

My paramour took off the television during our romance, and a telemarketer had called to introduce his wares. "I'm f-----! Don't disturb me." She slammed the phone.

We quarreled when I cloaked myself in Enid's sickness and kept away from her.

"When are you coming over, Lloyd?"

"I can't tell, Milly."

"You have to shit and fart before you come?"

"You know a lot about me."

"I have your X-ray, liar. You pretend that you don't love your wife. But as soon as you step into my house you are ready to run back home." She paused. "Is it love, or pity, for the sick?"

"Love."

"Why are you *prolonging* your misery?"

I stared at the black phone. "What do you mean?"

"Why do you give her *all* those unnecessary medications?"

"Her doctor recommended *Aricept* and *Namenda.*" I rushed for the pharmacy printouts of the common uses for *Namenda* and read it: *This medicine is a NMDA-receptor antagonist used to treat moderate to severe Alzheimer's-type dementia.*

Shocked by her inferred advice, yet I tempered my reply. I read another excerpt: *This medicine blocks excess activity of a substance in the brain called glutamate. Blocking glutamate may reduce the symptoms associated with Alzheimer's disease.*

I didn't understand the medical terms but I read on. I lengthened my explanation to prevent me erupting with vulgarity. "These medications are not cures for Alzheimer's. But my wife deserves them, and whatever medication is on the market, I'll find it for her. She has insurance!"

The import of Milly's question bowled me

into fear. *What could she be thinking*? I held the phone to my ear and waited.

"I'm just practical. My aunt's husband is sick for a long time. She wishes he dies, but she wants us to say so."

"Men who listen to women like you go to prison. Not me!" I hung up.

During our conversation, Enid held my shirt. She was in the advanced middle stage of Alzheimer's. As her sickness worsened, she lost her confidence. Wherever I went she followed me. When she didn't see me she hid in closets, in the bathtub, and behind the fridge. Once she forced herself underneath the bed, got stuck, and I knew her predicament when she squeaked like a mouse, trapped in fear, and pain. Immediately, I blocked every crevice below her bed and made it impossible for even her breath to pass underneath it. Next day I bought a large fridge to block the space where she once hid, and I also bought a captain bed with drawers at the bottom with not even space to put her fingers below the drawers.

Because Enid had held on to my shirt, I didn't want to answer Milly's question in code as I'd done before. There were times I had parsed my wife as a *common noun, neuter gender,* and hoped she had not understood that she was the subject of my covert conversation.

I swore that I would never call Milly again. But there were other people who were just as evil, verbally, to Enid. They spoke to me, in Enid's presence, of her, as if her Alzheimer's condition turned her into a dummy who couldn't understand what was said of her. I had told a malicious woman, as I looked into Enid's eyes, "My wife is smarter than you, even with her disease." My language was not civil.

I cooked corned beef and Uncle Ben's and prepared a fancy salad, and we ate every scrap of it that evening.

"It's time for your bath, Fats. Let me change your clothes."

"You like to bathe women to see their vaginas."

"Only yours I see."

"You have an *outside* child."

I was shocked by her answer. I presumed nightly baths resurrected "quirks of her memory," but Alzheimer's resumed its personality before she came out of the bathtub.

"Can I sleep here tonight?" She begged as

a homeless woman.

My eyes burned with hot tears whenever she said that. "Sure! I want you to sleep with me." I patted her space on the bed.

"No sex!" She was businesslike. She was again like the landlord who scolded her tenants about paying their rent on time.

"No sex, I promise." I, too, was businesslike for the purpose of hiding my laughter.

Every night didn't end with fun and frolic.

On February 5, 2003, I had tuned to C-Span. Secretary of State Colin Powell's address to the United Nations on Iraq's possession of WMD (weapons of mass destruction) was on. Enid was agitated because of another kind of WMD—"when men dither." I had screamed at her when she refused to let me change her wet pampers. Suddenly, pain lanced my head. I vaguely remembered my descent to the carpet. When I awoke—I don't know how long I was probably unconscious or fatigued from caretaking—she was crouched on my back, covered with clothes and hangers, in deep sleep, and snored aloud. I eased from under her. I hugged and kissed her tenderly as if it were the last day of our lives.

I shuddered to think what could have happened in the event of a fire that night. House

521, conjoined to **519**, had three fires since the landlady moved in. The last serious fire was on March 17, 2008. I was not at home.

The firemen burst our window blinds, opened all the windows, closed the front door and prevented the smoke from 521 from coming in by us. They took Enid out of her mechanical bed and put her in the wheelchair. June Fordrass, my friend, who volunteered her services that day because I didn't have a helper, pushed Enid by a window, wrapped her in blankets, and kept her warm until I came.

As I entered the vestibule, the smell of smoke choked me. I shouted, "Where's Fats? We had a fire here?"

"Next door. Your wife is okay. I didn't call you at the doctor's office because I was afraid you might have thought something bad had happened to your wife."

I hardly spoke that evening. I just thought of what could have been.

7

At nine o'clock in the morning of August 12, 2004, the phone rang. I did not answer. I thought it was Mr. Kwok, Tax Compliance Agent, who, on August 11, had come to our house to get my commitment to pay taxes owed to the State. I had already paid the Federal Government based on the sale of Enid's commercial property.

I prepared breakfast, set the table, and cut sausages in small pieces. I never trusted large pieces of meat. As a child, meat choked me. But the blow my mother gave my back dislodged the meat, but that blow with her fist could have killed me. We were about to eat when the phone rang again. I did not have caller ID.

"I hope Mr. Kwok is not calling today again. I've already told him that I will pay the State with my monthly Social Security checks. Hello!" I grunted.

"Who got you so mad?"

A familiar voice is heard. "Milly?"

"Who you thought it was?"

"I'm sorry." I laughed. Though I hadn't called her in many months because of the anger I harbored against her when she inferred I should discontinue my wife's medication, I was glad to hear her voice because I truly loved her.

We spoke as if we were strangers who looked for words to say. But I sensed she wanted to say something, and I lingered without saying a word.

"Are you there?"

"Yes."

"Please forgive me for what I said. I don't know where I got that hideous thought. What I really wanted to say...." She paused. I waited. "I wanted to say we, senior citizens, have to realize *our future is now* and we have to be careful."

"About what?"

"I wanted you to be careful when you are lifting your wife. You had told me that it was extremely difficult putting her in and taking her out of cabs when you took her to the doctor. Sometimes you had to ask the cabdriver to help you. You can hurt yourself, and both of you could end up in a wheelchair with prolonged illness. That is what I wanted to say, but somehow I said that other nonsense. Now that I explain myself better, do you forgive me?"

"I thought a bit.

"Would you forgive me, Lloyd?"

"Yes."

"Can I call you again?"

"Sure."

We became chummy again and called each other frequently, but I lost my trust in her. I also lost my trust in the law—not my complete trust--because of the behavior of two plain-clothes detectives.

8

We first lived on the parlor floor of a brownstone in Bedford Stuyvesant, a black neighborhood in Brooklyn. Enid and I were sitting with our door opened when the buzzer rang in Morse code. The tenant upstairs rushed down in pajamas and opened the front door for a man in business suit. "Do you have *it*?" the tenant asked.
"Yes."
"*It's* working?"
The businessman went into his briefcase, pulled *it* out, aimed *it* at the ceiling, looked at us, and said, "Just kidding."
Enid and I dragged our chairs, scuttled inside, and locked our doors. Enid's period came before its due date at the sight of the pointed gun.
That brownstone is now painted blue; its number remains *111*.
In April 1971, we bought **519**, an old-style-3-family-masonry structure, built in 1910, in West Flatbush. Our house is one of 15 houses on East 26

Street, bounded by Foster and Flatbush Avenues. Whenever I call the Mayor's representatives on 311 to complain about vehicles without number plates on the block and give them the boundaries of my block, they say, "Flatbush and Foster don't run parallel, so that is not the correct boundary." My nasty answer is always the same: "I live here! Not you!"

The three streets form a perfect triangle: East 26 is the height. Foster is the base, and Flatbush is the hypotenuse. On my block, traffic runs north. But traffic runs south on East 26, south of Flatbush.

All the houses are on the eastern side of the street. The western side displays the back walls of businesses and the back walls of two churches on Flatbush Avenue. The churches' main entrance is on Flatbush Avenue, but members can also make their entrance and exit from East 26. The pastors of both churches park on East 26 Street, an almost hidden street. The street sign was missing more often than not. A Nigerian Livery cab driver said, after I gave him a tip, "Man, you're not only cheap, but you live in a cove."

(Twenty years later I found out that one of the pastors who exited into the cove to get *its* car was a con artist. I will be referring to that con artist as Pastor X, and Pastor X's pronominal possessive would be "its." My reason for this is because later in this story I will be talking about a man pastor and a woman pastor, has or had, its church facing **519**. One of them came to rob Enid in the middle stage of AD.)

Before the sale of **519** was finalized, Enid and I visited the neighborhood three nights a week to observe if people sold drugs on our block. The sale of drugs was always on our minds because we didn't want our children to live in an environment where drugs are sold because we had seen the destruction of children who were lured by drug dealers in Bedford Stuyvesant. No one was on the block and not even the sound from an animal or a radio was heard as we walked slowly on the street. Only dim lights from the front rooms were seen on East 26th Street. "The lighting seems to be a code," Enid said. We couldn't wait for the closing of the deal to live in Flatbush on such a clean block with dimmed lights.

The sale went without a hitch, except the check I sent to the seller and the check he sent to me for escrow incidentals, bounced. The seller was a genial New York City policeman, and we chatted for an hour before the sale. His wife was a beautiful woman and very accommodating. Their dogs' scents remained in the house for months when they left. That didn't bother us because we now owned **519**.

On a mildly warm day we drove to our new abode. In Uncle Leon's car, packed like sardines, were Enid and our five children—Judy, Lloys, Taariq, Gail, and Nigel, four years old. The fourteen families and their tenants looked through their windows. Seven families came out and greeted us warmly. Harry, the spokesman, told us the block's rules for maintaining cleanliness. I told him that our family would adhere to them. He emphasized that we should always tie our garbage, bundle wood in small stacks, sweep the sidewalk, clean the snow 20 minutes after it fell, and tip the postman and sanitation crew at Christmas.

His advice became a serious instruction when I told him, "We came from Bedford Stuyvesant."

"Things are done differently here. Welcome to you and your family."

"Those rules will be followed, Harry."

Enid and I introduced ourselves to the other families who stood by.

Time went quickly. Harry peeped through his Venetian blinds to see if we put out our garbage as he advised. Enid and I pretended we didn't see him. We tied and re-tied the garbage bags tighter. We re-bundled the twigs separately, tightened the parcels of wood with two sets of twine. We swept from our porch to the boundary of the Sullivans', number 521, on the left, to the alleyway, on the right.

Harry and his family moved away within two years.

There was now an empty property, thirteen white families, and the Crooks family.

Our kids and the other kids became pals. The Pastalaqua family was their favorite hangout. Then the fights began: Crooks *versus* the Rest!

After Enid and I saw *The Godfather,* Enid's view of America changed. The clannish lifestyle of the Corleone family and their compatriots in that movie bothered her immensely. We prayed not to offend any of the white people on our block. No other movie in the history of our lives had touched a nerve as Mario Puzo's *The Godfather.*

We advised our children to be agreeable with the white kids and be courteous to their parents. Only three months on the block, Enid wondered if the Corleones and that sadistic Police Inspector's behavior in *The Godfather* was the norm. She altered her view quickly because of the kindness of neighbors.

Two white families rented the second floor of **519**. We met them there as tenants of the former owner. Tony lived in the front apartment; Vic lived in the rear. Enid was in charge of rental and repairs.

Vic, who, because of his last name, I assumed he was Italian-American. His hair was black and slicked as Tyrone Power's. He knocked out every built-in cabinet and left the wood on the floor. We were afraid to approach Vic about his deliberate damage despite the fact that the seller said everything will remain intact.

Vic and *The Godfather* became Enid's silent topics when the children slept.

One morning she told me of her dream. It was *Godfather* related.

Why?

She switched my names according to her mood: *Lloyd,* when she calls me as I'm known in New York by new friends, *Hollis,* as I'm known in Trinidad and Tobago.

"Hollis boy, let's take the damage Vic did to

our house. Have nothing to say to that man. You hear me? Tony is a darling. I hope he remains forever."

We shivered, however, when two New York policemen knocked on our door and questioned us about Tony's son. When the policemen left, Lloys said, "Rick sells stuff. That's why the police came here looking for him."

"How do you know?" Enid asked.

"Seems you forget I live here, too."

"Address me properly before I knock out your teeth. You hear me?"

"Sorry, mammy."

Both tenants left. The Irish family next door sold their property one month after. All the white families' houses were up for sale.

One of our worst experiences occurred in our basement. That was the first time I observed Enid's memory loss. I had never read about AD and about "plaques and tangles in the brain destroy brain cells and rob a person of memory and reasoning powers…and…*emotions affect the memory.*"

On a hot day in August, 1976, I, too, though not a neurologist, came to the conclusion in my research that "emotions affect the memory" because of the behavior of two plain-clothes detectives.

Enid had put Trish, three months old, to bed.

"Fats, Fats," I said. She did not give me time to finish my sentence.

"It's not yet bedtime to harass me for sex, so why are you calling me so often?"

"Because I'm always cooking, and I don't want you experimenting with cookbooks today."

"If you don't like my cooking, buy Chinese."

"Not today."

"I will cook enough carrot rice to last a month. Okay?"

"With chicken?"

"You know I don't eat that nasty bird."

"Stewed beef would be nice."

Carrot rice was on a low flame. Every wife should learn to cook Enid's carrot rice with the aroma that lingers. A marriage license should be given only after studying *The Enid Crooks Cookbook* not yet published. The diced carrot was seasoned with drops of Angostura bitters poured in as the rice simmered. Raisins were dropped in at intervals. She seasoned beef and covered it to marinate. I made the salad and was still looking for ingredients to add. We chatted, without interruption, because our hand-toy, Trish, was fast asleep.

Screams came from the basement. Taariq played his guitar in the living room. Judy, Lloys, and Gail watched cartoons, so we knew the screams were Nigel's.

The screams became louder. "Daddy, mammy, ain't I live here?"

Enid looked at me as she turned her aromatic pot with a large spoon. "That son of yours has no behavior."

Whenever the children got good school reports they were *her* children, but whenever they misbehaved they were *mine*.

Nigel's screams were ignored. We knew he was in the basement, probably unhinging something. His pastime was destroying things. We seldom gave our children toys, but the few he got never remained hinged after the first hour.

"Daddy, mammy, ain't I live here?" His question was louder. Deep fear was now evident in his voice.

We dropped everything in hand and rushed to the basement.

When he heard our footsteps he barely whispered, "Mammy, daddy, ain't I live here?"

Two plainclothes detectives—I'd seen them in the neighborhood before—had their guns placed at each side of Nigel's temple.

Enid screamed with a quartet of sentences: "That's my son! He lives here! He's nine years old! What he did?"

When I'm confused, I speak a kind of syllabic gibberish interspersed with undecipherable English. I'm sure the two detectives did not understand what I said.

One detective said, calmly, as if he were satisfied with his heinous performance, "Since you people moved into the neighborhood, it is deteriorating, and there's always trouble."

"We don't cause any trouble." I must have made other remarks.

Enid cupped her belly as if preventing a miscarriage. She lost her balance, and I held her firmly to prevent her from crashing to the ground.

I vividly remember the sight of the two detectives as they moved their guns from Nigel's temple, raised their pants folds, put their firearms in holsters strapped to their ankles, and walked out of the basement.

They drove off in an unmarked car. I locked the basement door to the street that was opened on that almost fatal day, and kept it locked up to this day.

The seasoned beef was never cooked. Our children ate the carrot rice without meat.

That night Enid lost her memory. She had forgotten the words of *The Savior With Me*, her signature hymn. She tried to sing it but had forgotten it. She did not remember *The Lord's Prayer*, a prayer she had recited when she knelt with her mother and grandmother. That prayer was recited nightly with her own children before they went to bed.

"*Our Father...Our Father...Our Father....*"

That's all she remembered.

Her prayer was a disconnected set of words: "*Dear Lord, I thank you. Their guns...their guns... If their guns had....*"

She had forgotten how to make a sentence. She went into her drawer for two scarves. She knotted them. She tied her belly almost the same way a Trinidad-and-Tobago unlicensed midwife tied a pregnant woman after she delivered her baby to flatten her stomach. Enid rolled the scarves instead. As a boy, my mother often rolled an empty flour bag and tied below her belly to relieve the stress from my father's infidelity.

Enid went to bed, and shook sporadically in her sleep. And I couldn't help thinking, did "emotions affect her memory" that night because of what the two plain-clothes detectives did to our son, Nigel: Putting their guns on his temple because he was *playing in his basement*?

Then myriads of thoughts collided in my brain, and I asked myself pertinent and impertinent questions of why those two white, plain-clothes detectives did that to our nine-year-old son: Is it because we are the only black family on the block and one of our children fought with one of the white kids on the block and beat him up; and the white kids told those two white detectives to come and frighten us? That couldn't be because all my children were friendly with the other children, and there was not a fight on the block at that time. Is it because those two white detectives are probably rogue cops who hate to see the block is changing? Did they come in our unlocked basement to frighten us because we are Johnnies-come-lately, and we don't know U.S. laws? Are they not New York City detectives, but frauds? Couldn't be, because I've seen them before in an official capacity? Why? Why? Then I thought of an incident that I had witnessed in Bedford Stuyvesant at the corner of Nostrand and Gates Avenues where two white policemen had badly beaten up a white guy who was leading a march with only black people. The talk on the street was: *Those two white cops thought that white guy should not be leading any black march; he is out of place.* Then I thought of what had happened in the South in the forties to black people. But we are way up North in the seventies! My mind drifted to the first advice that Marian Sutherland had given me: "Hollis, you are not in Trinidad and Tobago where everyone will know you worked in the Prime Minister's Office and you were also a Parliament Reporter and Enid was also a civil servant. You and Enid are *just* numbers in a file here in America. Another thing: Hollis, I know of Caribbean men's heat in their pants. Don't go chasing white girls—worse still, don't go in their neighborhood at nights." The weight on my thoughts gave me insomnia that night.

Thirty eight years have passed, but Taariq and I find ourselves discussing the behavior of those two detectives. Then he rewinds into his junior high school years when he and Nigel had to run from white boys after school and many times dropped their school bags to develop speed from the pack.

I told Taariq "two swallows don't make a summer," and two bad detectives don't make New York City constabulary. He replied: "Sir, when I served as a juror some years ago, one of those white boys who chased me after school, who is now a policeman, gave evidence on the accused, a black man. After swearing in with his hand on the Bible, I looked straight into his eyes, and he looked down when our eyes met. Surely, he remembered me and what he and his friends did to black boys after school was over."

"Am sure he's a changed man now, Taariq."

"I hope so."

I wanted to ask him what was the verdict in that case against the black defendant, but knowing my son, I knew he would not have told me.

9

With the new gentrification of East 26th Street, trees proudly fly foreign flags. Nailed to the three remaining trees are flags of Jamaica, Haiti, Grenada, St. Vincent and the Grenadines, Trinidad and Tobago, Barbados, Guyana, Costa Rica, Panama, United States, and other countries. The constant noises of the new inhabitants flutter the flags more than the summer breeze.

"Daddy, how do you live in this noise? This noise wasn't here in 1971 when we moved in as children. When I came from South Africa last year it wasn't this bad."

"Lloys, I asked Dwayne Arbuckle to become the President of the Block Association since your mother's illness. Somehow, he's afraid of the task. He came and looked for your mother and brought pampers for her twice. He's very fond of the senior citizens on the block. But he wants no part of being a block watchman. He said that he's tired of trying to keep the block clean. Dumpers come at nights and unload their garbage here. Stolen cars are also deposited here late at nights and your mother wakes me up to see."

"And what are people doing to the trees? I played under those trees!" Lloys stepped on the porch and looked at a dying hedge maple fissured with nail stabs to hold foreign flags. Least prominent on that tree was an American flag, 4-by-3-inch, on a two-inch pole. It is similar in size to the one George Foreman waved in his 1968 Heavyweight Boxing Olympic victory in Mexico City, and that little flag had no space to flutter proudly in the wind. That 4-by-3 Old Glory was housed in a milk crate nailed to the hedge maple. I gave sufficient money for the purchase of a large American flag but the tree decorator bought that size. A concerned American nailed his large flag to the trunk of another tree sometime later.

Cynthia Jerry, founder and first president of the East 26 Street Block Association, moved to Florida, and Enid Crooks assumed the duty of president in the eighties. President Crooks was energetic and innovative. She organized block parties, block cleanups, and meetings in our basement and backyard. She impressed on all that we should keep our block clean and enter the Borough President's block beautification competition. She was never successful.

"That bitch in that house thinks she owns the block. I dropped a piece of paper, and she told me to pick it up as if I'm her child. I wanted to kick that bitch." The young man looked at our building as he spoke to his friend.

"If you knew her sons, Snake and J-Quan (street names for Taariq and Nigel), you won't talk that shit. They'd beat you down. Mrs. Crooks is a nice lady," his companion said.

The two young men didn't know who I was when I trailed their footsteps. Everyone knew Mrs. Crooks. Mrs. Fox, in House 523, met me on the subway for the first time and wagered a bet that I didn't live at **519**. "I know Mrs. Crooks and her children, not you."

Mrs. Fox had a good reason to believe I lived elsewhere. I never looked out at the commotions on the block, and the commotions are frequent now. She didn't know me because I got up early, left English and math homework for my children, and walked in one direction every day. I returned home late at night after working overtime or after gallivanting in the city.

Enid's block presidency was made easy with

the help of Mary James and Felicita Raynor. All three whom I call *the Three Queens* were in their prime then, only Enid was alive. Felicita, Jamaican-American, was a housewife who spent long hours in her flower garden and callalloo patch. Callalloo is a plant, and from it cooks make a tasty Caribbean dish. She looked out for the street mechanics and dumpers. Her Jamaican patois had blockbusters scampering like flitted flies. I remember the day she chased out a businessman: "Teef, get outta me yard! Ah say get outta me yard, now, teef!" He had given her an estimate for repairs to be done to her house, and she thought his estimate was ridiculously overpriced; and he was a thief trying to con her. She knows a reasonable estimate because her husband was in the building trades.

Mary, 96 pounds, or less, a psychiatric nurse, was diplomatic as they come. She made friends with everyone. She got over her message to the tenants who put out their garbage in paper bags to the attraction of dogs and cats.

Felicita, before her death at 96, had neither bark nor bite as formerly. She was cared for by her son, Myles, "a good son," as she had described him to me. Myles was good to Enid and me, too. Many times he shoveled our snow and cut our fence, free of charge. He always bestowed God's blessings on us.

Mary died at 81. She was my favorite neighbor, and we discussed our children. "Mr. Crooks, my children are all good children. But Harriet (nicknamed Tweet) is a blessing to me. She sees to it that I am on top of my health." Tweet always seeks our interest. She, too, has shoveled our snow. She calls us "Mamma Crooks, Papa Crooks." She holds a Master's Degree in Social Work and the road she walked for that degree is a success story for her, her family, and East 26, the block she and Myles still try to upkeep, but without success.

Enid, 77, doesn't know that City Hall and the Borough President still address letters to her as President of the Block Association. Her present state is eons away from when she attended Logos Bible College and came home and said, "Hollis, read my essay, type it, and learn something about God."

Every Thanksgiving Day she fed people in homeless shelters. An exchange between her and a homeless man from the Marcus Garvey Avenue Armory shelter showed her kindness and firmness.

"Give me a plate of food, babe!" the

homeless man demanded.

She handed dinners to everyone, except to him. Her members were afraid of him for he threatened people in the neighborhood. Her members also thought he would have knocked her aside and would have taken as many plates as he wished. Probably he knew the Trinidad and Tobago lingo, "Monkey knows what tree to climb."

He studied her calmness, and said, "Pastor Crooks, I'm sorry for calling you *babe*. Please, give me a plate of food."

She handed him two plates, and said, "Not because you are homeless you shouldn't be respectful. Not even my husband calls me *babe*. And he helped me clean four crates of collard greens so that you can eat today."

As glib as she was, her memory faded intermittently. She had asked countless times if I'd eaten. I eventually held a dirty paper plate in my hand to show that I had eaten.

She kept her appointments with her prison ministry and cried after each visit. In hindsight, I felt her tears were not for the prisoners' plight only, but that she had done due diligence on her brain and didn't want her family to know her fear of becoming an Alzheimer's patient as her father. She had searched for him many nights in the rain in Trinidad and cried when she brought him home.

"Father is my life," was her swansong.

10

CNN's *Larry King's Interview* at 9:00 P.M. was a "must see" when our children lived with us. When they moved away, I discussed the interviews with Enid. I knew she did not understand what took place, but I engaged her anyhow. She was always great company. Whenever I was away I missed her dearly.

Larry King's relaxed style encourages his guests to loosen up. He props his chin, fatherly-like, as if waiting to hear a child's story and uses his comforting demeanor to elicit the truth that the child might not have otherwise told.

Enid was not cranky when King interviewed the former First Lady Nancy Reagan. Other nights when she was, I calmed her with food or fruits. She looked at me when I ate alone as if she hadn't eaten for the day. Sometimes I hid to eat or made sure that we ate together to avoid her hungry look. That look became an art form.

For the Nancy Reagan interview, Enid did

not want fruit or food, *a good omen,* I thought. Still, I peeled a banana, pulled down the skin an inch, and bit once into that bent, yellow, Chiquita. Its shipping number was barely visible.

The interview began.

Nancy Reagan spoke in glowing terms of her husband, President Ronald Reagan, who was stricken with Alzheimer's disease. From childhood I was never a Reagan fan and hated when my on-and-off friend, Kelvin said, "Ronald Reagan is better looking than Robert Taylor."

"Never happened!" I said. That was the hip slang in Fyzabad when one doubted the other, and most times my doubt was complimented with obscenity. "Reagan could never be @%$&* good looking as RT."

A new kind of love for President Reagan developed when he became an Alzheimer's patient. I became his new fan, and he became my hero when he spoke to his beloved country and the world, and intimated his "long goodbye." His words, "I now begin the journey that will lead me into the sunset of life," moved me to tears, and I thought of my wife's ill health.

Commercials came on. I went into my medicine cabinet for my prescription, sleeping pill, *5421*, but I changed my mind. I remembered *5421* makes me incoherent in minutes. Once Lloys called from South Africa, and she did not understand what I said. She then called her sister, Gail. "What is wrong with my father?" Gail replied: "Never call him A*5421* (after taking *5421*) because he speaks nonsense. Always call him B*5421* (before taking *5421*).

In the commercial break I spoke to Enid. "Fats, that was Nancy Reagan speaking to Larry King. She'll be coming on again after the commercial break."

It was neither here nor there with Fats because she knew neither of them.

The interview resumed.

King locked his eyes with the former First Lady's, and asked: "What should people know who hear this about a relative, a wife, a husband, a mother, a father? What advice can the caregiver give another caregiver?"

The camera zoomed on Mrs. Reagan. She looked radiant in yellow.

She replied: "Well, that's hard to answer, Larry. You just get up each day and put one foot in front of the other and go. You know, each day is different."

King said, "There are hospitals that specialize in just treating Alzheimer's patients. You would never do that?"

She answered, "Oh no! Oh no! Never! Never! No! No! He's going to stay at home."

I phoned my friend, June, who lives in Bedford Stuyvesant. Before I said a word, she said, "I listened to the interview."

"I was emotional," I said. "The effect of the disease was one thing, but Mrs. Reagan's love for President Reagan carried the interview... especially the way she refused to put her husband in a facility. I, too, will never put Fats into a nursing home." I paused, and June knew that I was choking up.

"Hollis, sometimes we have no choice. I loved Uncle Dee very much. He was my husband for 50 years. But I had no other choice but to put him in Kingsbrook Nursing Home. He was later transferred to the hospital ward. He was 75 years old when he died. He lost both legs from diabetic complications, and he had a heart attack. I suspect that *other* thing was approaching."

"That was really a difficult task for you."

"At age 70, long before Uncle Dee was put in the nursing home, he said in the saddest way,

'June, it seems I'm getting *that thing*. I went to the store to buy cigarettes, and I couldn't find my way back home. A man brought me back.' Uncle Dee called Alzheimer's *that thing*. Though he didn't die from Alzheimer's, he hated the thought of it."

"Fats, too, never called the word *Alzheimer's*. What eventually made you put Uncle Dee in Kingsbrook? Couldn't you hold out longer? The City was giving you help."

"My husband was sickly homophobic. He preferred our only son was a bank robber and shot by the police *than* if our son were a successful homosexual living like a king in Hollywood. Whenever the City sent male nurses to attend to Uncle Dee, he screamed bloody murder. He would not let them touch him. He thought the mere idea that they were males they could be men lovers. It was too much for me alone to handle. I had no choice but to put him in the nursing home. You know Uncle Dee's ways since you were a boy. You know how Caribbean men are when it comes to another man touching their private parts, even if that man is a male nurse doing his job?"

I did not answer.

June kept talking of her love for Uncle Dee: How he married her when she was 17 years old. "He was the only man that I had loved. And I loved him at first sight at the age of 14. Like Mrs. Reagan, I, too, had to get up each day and put one foot in front of the other and go on. You have to do the same, Hollis."

The hot phone in my ear reminded me: *What is man, that thou art mindful of him?* That biblical line, taken from Psalm 8, Verse 4, was one of Pastor Crooks's favorite themes.

"Are you there, Hollis?"

"Yes, June."

"You, too, have to put one foot in front of the other and go forward with God. Even my daughter, Patricia, an RN, couldn't handle her father and advised me that I could no longer take care of him at home."

"I would never put Fats in a nursing home, unless, unless...." I didn't end the sentence.

Time had no connection with my thoughts. My thoughts became current when Enid left me and put a bar of soap into her mouth. I took the soap from her mouth and gave her the banana that I had bitten and left on the kitchen counter.

11

I was playing the piano when mammy interrupted me to know if I would become an Anglican Minister.

"How was it, Blackboy?" That's how my mother and godmother called me. The genesis of that nickname was unkind, but then, if a parent or a godparent called you by any name you had to abide by it, or swallow your saliva if you didn't like it. I got to like my nickname eventually.

I had returned from an interview with Fyzabad Anglican Church's lay-reader, Harold M. Telemaque. He was my headmaster at Fyzabad Intermediate Anglican School. We met again when he became an Inspector of Schools, and I was a stenographer in the Department of Education, in San Fernando, the second largest town in Trinidad, also referred to as "the industrial capital of Trinidad and Tobago." He told me that the Bishop needed young men for the seminary in Codrington College, Barbados, and he would like to recommend me.

"Sir, I'm too worldly for that."

Mr. Telemaque, a tall, black, and handsome man, nicknamed "the Buge," was my idol. But when I was in his class I hated him. He had corrected my essay titled WHAT YOU'D LIKE TO BE WHEN YOU GROW UP? Nearly every class teacher had us writing that *stupid* essay as if the boys had a crystal ball in their short pants pockets and the girls had it under their skirts.

He corrected my essay with red ink and lectured me on grammar and syntax. Then he flung my copy book. The pages went haywire, and my classmates laughed aloud.

"What the hell is wrong with you?" I didn't know when those words came out. I never answered any of my teachers like that before.

"What you said, boy?"

"Are you deaf? You are no Buge for me." My answers got feistier every time the students chuckled.

That was the worst flogging I'd gotten in my school life. Worse still, I could not go home and tell my mother why those marks were on my body because Mr. Telemaque, head teacher extraordinaire, and Tubal Uriah Butler, the one-man trade union of the oilfield workers in the thirties and forties, did no wrong.

The Buge and I drifted into casual chitchat, and he drove home the point why I should become an Anglican minister. I told him had he known what I did when a boy under his tutelage, apart from when I was rude to him, he would have expelled me from school.

He laughed. His laughter was a musical cough. What was good about the Buge was that he listened to people's problems, and he knew something private about most of us. He was well informed of the villagers and by the villagers.

"Why don't you want to become an Anglican minister, Hollis?"

"Sir, I don't think I qualify."

"You are afraid if you go away you'd lose Meena?"

"I have already lost her." *Who the hell told him that*?

"How?"

"Her East Indian father doesn't want any black man marrying his daughters."

"Meena's mother is a black woman, only her complexion is light. He can have our black women, and his half-Indian daughter is off limit to us? Aren't you fighting it, Hollis?"

"No, sir."

He looked at me. "Why?" He saw I was not interested in talking about a lost love.

He reverted to his original topic. "The Bishop would be interested in getting young men like you. Why not give it a thought?"

"I've grown to distrust church teachings after I attended Freethinkers meetings."

"You go to atheist John Jules's meetings?"

"Yes, sir."

"Why do you distrust church teachings?"

"At seven years old, my mother could not afford to keep me with her so she had sent me to live with my godmother. I ate my godmother's sugar because I was hungry. Godmother was a devoutly religious woman. She took me to church day and night." I stopped.

"What she said?"

"Blackboy, you are a thief! God will never forgive you for this. If you continue to thief, the Devil will burn you in everlasting fire."

Mr. Telemaque looked at me.

"I had believed that church teaching of fear from my godmother, and it affected me deeply. My agnostic studies helped me overcome my fear about heaven and hell, and I now believe heaven and hell are on earth."

"Was your godmother a nice lady?"

"She was the best. She loved me dearly."

"You believe in God?"

"My way."

I swiveled on the piano stool and smiled at my mother after I related how my interview went with Mr. Telemaque.

"Blackboy, that smile means?"

"I'm not going to be an Anglican minister. Let me help you with the goods, mammy."

"I knew the Buge couldn't rope you in as he did Kenny Forrester." She dumped a bleeding fish in the kitchen sink. The fisherman had a fresh catch. "I have a *lowdown* for you."

"What's the *lowdown*, mammy?"

"A new girl, a pretty girl, is working in the post office."

"You got mail?"

"Nobody knows us."

I pretended I was not interested in any *new* girl.

Five minutes later I left on the pretense that I was going to see Alston Noble, but detoured to the post office.

As I walked to the post office mammy's love for me crossed my mind. I was about to turn around and go back home and forget everything about "the new girl, a pretty girl, is working in the post office." But I knew mammy wanted me to see her. Instantly, I remembered one of her testaments of her love for me:

Her inked testament was written to Wilfred D. Best, Headmaster of Forest Reserve E.C. School. That was my second primary school. I was ten years old. I felt like Moses who carried the Tablet for the Israelites as I walked three-and-three-quarter miles to school. Barefooted on the hot pitch, I hoped the testament in my book bag would not cause me shame.

The asphalt felt hotter than usual and every now and then I walked on the dewy grass and cooled my soles. I dare not reach late to school because Mr. Best flogged latecomers and said, "Latecomers never make good citizens." He made us recite the school motto after prayers: *We learn that we may serve.*

As my feet touched the first treadle of the post office steps, my life went in reverse. I relived the day that I took mammy's testament of her love for me, written in black ink, with a nib tied with thread to a piece of stick. She had dipped the nib into an old bottle of Parker ink that had become lumpy.

My mother's testament is not verbatim, but I remember the main details 67 years later as if it were written today:

Dear Mr. Best: Good morning. When Hollis is not at school, he is in the garden (fields) working with me, planting corn, rice, and ground provision. I did not keep him away from school this week because he is doing his term test. He wants to come first in test, and you are preventing him.

You gave him NAUGHT for the duck he did for woodwork. You called him a LIAR and a CHEAT who found that old, lumpy, dirty duck in the rubbish. Hollis is not good in drawing, but he drew that duck on a piece of cardboard and cut it out. He placed the cutout on a piece of old board, traced it, and then used a hacksaw blade to cut his crooked duck out of the board.

The duck may not look pretty as those ducks swimming in TLL ponds, but Hollis duck is his own woodwork duck.

He spent days sandpapering his duck. We are poor people, and do not have money to buy paint to paint the duck white and pretty. I begged Mr. Marshall, my neighbor, for some paint. The paint he gave me was dry. I poured a little

kerosene into the paint to melt it, but the paint was insufficient to paint both sides of the duck, so I added a LITTLE MUD to the paint, and that is why the duck looks old, dirty, and lumpy.
   I watched Hollis work on his duck day and night. If you give him NAUGHT for his duck, that will not be fair because he made that duck with his own hands. He did not find it in the rubbish.

Yours truly,
Leoni Crooks

In that flashback, I had reached to school before the bell rang. I hurried upstairs, and rested the letter on Mr. Best's desk.
   School assembled. We stood and said prayers. After prayers, if Mr. Best rang the bell twice, it meant to sit; once, meant to remain standing for an announcement.
   He rang once. "I have an important letter from a parent."
   Mr. Best lived in Trinidad Leasehold Limited's private quarters on the school premises. From his house he could almost jump into the school. He wore a white shirt, seamless, as if it were washed, starched, and ironed by his maid twenty

seconds before he walked in. His wiry hair, evenly Brylcreamed, scented the room. His brown trousers looked foreign. My stepfather never wore that kind of clothes to work. He wore blue dock or khaki.

Mr. Best pulled mammy's letter from his drawer like Mandrake the magician, and read it slowly. He never looked at me until he stressed the words: Leoni Crooks.

He addressed his audience. "I wish other parents are interested in their children as Leoni Crooks."

He rang the bell twice. Students and teachers sat. In those days, when 100 children were in attendance, Archdeacon Banks gave us a church holiday. When he ended my mother's letter with such praise, it was as if it were another church holiday for me.

My woodwork grade was a perfect score. Still I didn't beat Sheila Henry. I came second in that term test.

As I stepped into the post office my daydream ended. I whistled *The Nearness of You* and walked to the new employee's station.

"Good afternoon. Are there any letters for Hollis Crooks or for Lloyd Crooks?"

"I'll check the mailbox, *only* if you tell me

the name of that tune, and teach me." She smiled.

"*The Nearness of You.*" I did not answer the second part of her question.

"Is Leoni Crooks related to you?"

"Mammy? I mean my mother."

"She was here earlier."

"If she had told me there were no letters for me, I would not have come."

"I'm glad you came. How could I get a copy of that tune?"

"Come with me."

"Where?"

"To my house."

"Give me half an hour to balance my ledger."

She was out in less than half an hour.

She introduced herself. "I'm Enid Bain. I knew of you before now."

"How come?"

"I work in the post office. Connecting people with names is my business."

"Then you already know in which half-board-half-mud house I live?"

"I'm not that good."

I knew she was the city type. My premonition: She either lived in Port of Spain, or its close environs. Her smile was beautiful. Her two front teeth, joined with spliced gold, enhanced her beauty. That dust of gold in people's mouths at that exact spot as in hers was the in-thing in cosmetic surgery in Trinidad and Tobago in the fifties. Even if I could have afforded it, or liked gold in my mouth, I was afraid of the dentist's drill.

Never had I seen such a beautiful smile flashed my way. Immediately, I wished I could kiss her the way Meena and I kissed when we traveled on the TGR bus to school. We kissed when the driver was not looking in his rearview mirror.

Fyzabad girls dressed casually during the work week. They dolled up beautifully when they went to parties, weddings, and soirées. Their hairdos were similar: ninety nine percent of them became *hot-iron blondes* or *coal-pot Douglas,* a nickname given to black women with kinky hair turned straight or curly with hot combs. *Dougla* is coined to mean the offspring of a Black man and Indian woman, *vice versa.* Their children usually have straight or curly hair.

Enid wore designer clothes that day. Her hair was poodle styled, short and curled like a poodle dog's. Later I learned Mom rebuked her for cutting her long hair in "that whore style." Trust Mom for her acrid tongue that Enid acquired to a tee. In her earlobes were gold earrings. She wore a beige dress, one cut, fitted to her knees. With my admiration, she said, "My sister, Sylvie, is a seamstress."

"How long have you been here?"

"For two interesting weeks."

"You are more attractive than mammy's description."

"Miss Crooks told you about me?"

"She looks out for me."

"What else she said?"

"She hopes you don't open people's mail and read them as the other clerks do."

"So you people know our nasty habit?"

I held her hand and guided her away from fresh cow dung. "Would you believe there was a dam here as big as a lake with lilies and alligators? When I was a boy, I came at nights with a flashlight to see alligators' eyes."

"Where?"

"Right here. Right where we are walking. And this log that we are walking on is known as *The Bridge*. Boys learned everything about girls and sex on this log."

"You, too?"

I smiled.

"Who was the teacher?"

"The boy who was the oldest that day, and we all got our sex knowledge from Uncle Dee."

"I heard about him the first day I came to work in the post office. I heard he has countless women. What else you know about us in the post office?"

"Probably you've read letters coming to and from me."

"And if I didn't?"

"You must! That's your initiation to be accepted as a true member of the clan, otherwise the postmistress would have you transferred in a week on a charge of insubordination."

"You really know what takes place in Fyzabad Post Office. Now I want to keep my job and stay in Fyzabad as long as possible."

"See!"

"You want to hear the truth?"

"Yes."

"I know about your girlfriend and about her East Indian father who hates black men."

"How do you know about them?"

"I work in the post office. I didn't know who you were, but I know who you are now. I read those letters that you wrote your girlfriend."

"Prove it."

"Her name is Meena. She wrote you when you were vacationing in Mason Hall, Tobago. You were bathing in Courland River when your cousin Irvine received her letter and brought it to you. She told you in that letter her father...You want me to continue?"

"You surely passed your initiation. The postmistress will keep you."

"Do you still want me to follow you home for the words of that song?"

"Are you always that truthful?"

"Ask my parents about me. They would tell you that every year I got a flogging from Mom for dancing in the carnival bands and leaving my little sisters, Versil and Pearl, with a lady who roasted corn by the roadside. I knew I was going to get a good whipping from Mom, but I didn't care because I enjoyed myself when I jumped up with short shorts in the bands."

"Why didn't you take your little sisters to jump up in the carnival bands with you?"

"They would have seen my boyfriend, and Mom hated him. She warned me before I left home, 'Enid, keep away from that naked-big-mouth-ugly Horace Gordon.'"

"How you got out of the house with those micro shorts?"

"I put my carnival clothes with my sisters' playthings."

"What a genius babysitter?"

"*Where there's a will, there's a way.*"

We walked inside my parents' house. The doors were never locked. At nights we pushed a bench and blocked the front door. That was a good method because as Paul and I stepped into adolescence and came in late at nights, mammy was tired of getting up to open the creaky door so that it would not wake up our stepfather.

"Mammy, I brought a stranger to see you."

"I'm frying fish. You brought the pretty girl in the post office?"

"How did you know I went to the post office?"

"I'm just guessing. Bring her in the kitchen."

"I am looking for the sheet music for *The Nearness of You.*"

"She's going to sing for half of your dinner?"

"Mr. Joe's, not mine!"

"Who's Mr. Joe?" Enid inquired.

"My stepfather. His full name is Joseph Sears. I ate his dinner many nights and pretended that I didn't know the difference with his dinner in a white ware plate that mammy kept away from other dishes and mine in a red enamel plate."

"Did you get a whipping?"

"My belly was full, so I didn't care."

"Pretty girl in the post office, did Blackboy tell you that if he passes the Civil Service exam he'll be leaving me to go and work in the Prime Minister's Office in Port of Spain?" Mammy boasted nonstop about me.

"He had me spilling my guts but he said nothing."

"Mammy, she came here to sing. Please excuse us."

I led her to the upright piano. Her voice made me believe John Garfield's words in *Golden Boy,* "There's no war in music." It was the first time that I'd met someone who could sing all the parts to a pop song, effortlessly, and changed it into a propulsive flow of calypso rhythms. I couldn't find the chord changes to match her range, and I never knew how to play a calypso, on the beat. Mrs. Alleyne, my classical music teacher, never allowed calypso playing in her class. There was another deterrent for my not being able to play a calypso.

"Were you born in Trinidad?"

"Right here in Fyzabad."

"And you can't play a calypso beat?"

"No." I closed the piano and looked for conversations.

"Why are you working in a post office? You should be on *Radio Trinidad* singing, announcing, or serving coffee until you get your big break."

"I sang on *Radio Trinidad* when I was in SAGS (St. Augustine Girls' High School).

"Who taught you harmonies?"

"Father. He plays the piano, too."

"You play, too?"

"I'm hoping one day you'd teach me."

I did not know whether that was a statement, foresight, or question, so I did not answer that question. "I hope I'll have the privilege of meeting Father."

"Not before meeting Willy the Tank."

"Who's that?"

"My brother."

"What's so special about him?"

"He's my real buddy, more than my other brother, Vernon. When Vernon didn't want to offer you a bite in his snowball, he'd spit on it and ask, 'You still want it, Enid?'"

"I did that too when schoolmates begged

me. There had to be a better reason why you preferred Willy the Tank."

"Every Friday we fought as a team since I was in grade four." She laughed heartily before she began her story.

"Why?"

"The children who reported me to Mr. Doyle, the headmaster, and made me get a whipping for talking in class, had to pay."

"Weren't they bigger than you?"

"Yes."

"Then how come you beat them?"

She told her story and laughed all through it.

After school the children took their favorite route home and passed by the lofty Samaan whose trunk could hide an elephant. Friday fights under the large branches were egged on by the words, "Heave! Heave!" As Enid hit her challengers first and the children shouted, "Heave! Heave!" Willy the Tank appeared from behind the tree trunk.

Murchison, the prefect extraordinaire, the new kid in her class didn't know Enid's game otherwise he would never have reported her misbehavior to Mr. Doyle. The other mistake he made was to report her talkativeness on a Thursday.

On that Thursday, Mr. Doyle had put her to stand on a bench with her hands raised for the greater part of the afternoon. Every opportunity Murchison got he made monkey face to her. That was his way of showing he had authority as the class prefect. Enid told the Tank of Murchison's sin. The Tank meant vengeance on Friday for sinners—children who reported his beloved sister to the headmaster for talking in class.

Boys and girls walked behind Enid to her favorite spot. By the Samaan they shouted the code words. The poor-Murchison kid didn't know he was walking the route of hapless fate.

She reached her earmarked spot that witnessed so many crucifixions. She punched Murchison in his back and ran to the base of the Samaan.

Murchison dropped his books and dashed behind her. Willy the Tank appeared. He pushed Murchison to the ground and said to his sister, "Kick him, E! Kick him, E!"

E kicked him.

"More, E!"

She kicked Murchison until her little feet were tired. Her Bata shoes, too; they left her feet.

School children shouted, "Heave! Heave!" They, too, were tired from just looking at Enid Bain in action.

The Tank and his sister walked home, and the school children discussed who was going to be Enid's victim next Friday.

While Enid laughed about her fighting Fridays, I cringed at the thought of Hugh D's brutality every Friday, the Tucker boys, too, as I walked home from school. At times I wanted to walk with a penknife to stab them, but the thought of mammy's shame, had I done so, prevented me from applying street justice.

"What's Willy's occupation now—a bouncer in a disco bar, or a wing man?"

I didn't force her for an answer because she laughed nonstop. Somehow though an odd feeling came over: *Is she an undercover detective? How could she know of my love affair with Meena and other private matters in my life? Reading my letters in the post office could only tell her so much. Was she sent to the post office to spy on me?*

Villagers had intimated that strange men, not Fyzabadians, inquired about me: about my character, my friends; "all kind of crazy questions they asked about you, Hollis." Mr. Frederick, the Vice Principal of Fyzabad Intermediate Anglican School had told me a man inquired about me. I went to Sonny, my tailor, to listen to the *Voice of America*. "Hollis, are you in big trouble with the police? A man came and asked me crazy questions about you."

I retraced a past observation: When I left my job in San Fernando, a man had shadowed me to the bus terminus. He took the TGR bus and came off my stop. I'd never seen him before. I knew all or nearly all the people in Fyzabad. Better still, I knew everyone who walked up Gower's Well Road where I lived or drew water from the well. When I turned into my mud track, he walked up the hill. He was not a numbers runner. I knew them all. He didn't sell milk. My mother bought milk from every milk vendor, and still owed most of them. He wasn't dating any of the women on the hill because Faye would have told me. We were buddies.

Was he spying on me?

Is Enid spying on me now?

Mammy put our dinner on the table, and I looked at Enid to see if she ate like a spy.

How does a spy eat?

"Why are you looking at me like that? You want back your mother's food?"

"Just curious at the way you made yourself

comfortable."

"When I take you to Mom and Father and they give you dinner, you won't be comfortable?"

"I guess so."

I excused myself from the table, went to the backyard, and mammy kept her company. I heard their laughter. It was not a surprise because mammy was an excellent host.

I took Enid to the beginning of the steep hill that lead to Miss Vie's boarding house.

From the top of the hill, she shouted, "Blackboy, why did you thief Mr. Joe's dinner?"

"Because his food had all the meat."

Mammy had told her tidbits of my life. When I looked up again, and I didn't see her, I felt she had slipped and fell to the other side of the hill. I rushed up the hill. She sat on the grass and laughed nonstop. Her beautiful dress was soiled. Her laughter was more important than her dress.

I picked her up. "Where did you learn to laugh and throw yourself in the mud?"

"Father does the same thing. But when I think of the ingenious lies you gave your mother after you stole your stepfather's dinners, that's what made me laugh this much."

"You never stole when you were a kid?"

"I played in Gamma's cashew sale money. She left it where I could find it. That was not stealing."

"Who is Gamma?"

"My grandmother. She was a cane farmer and a preacher with her own church. She had lots of money."

I led her to her doorstep. "May I kiss you, city girl?"

"You may, country boy."

I ran down the hill, and whistled *The Nearness of You*.

We became lovers. Yet I doubted my true love for her. We went to parties, dances, movies, mountain climbing, and I loved the clothes she wore. Meena was no longer on my mind. Enid's boyfriend, Horace Gordon, who jilted her and married a teenaged girl, was no longer on her mind either.

I visited her family in Tunapuna. They lived in a beautiful 4-bedroom house. The bedrooms were painted in calypso colors. "I chose those colors," Enid said. I almost forgot I came to see her parents when I saw the Cayenne guavas hanging over the verandah. I pulled the branches and ate guavas ravenously. I pushed the worms and seeds aside. Father and Mom were happy to see me, and so was I. We chatted a little, and Mom scrutinized me. Father just grinned, and I knew he liked me. I had worn gabardine trousers and a grayish shirt. I still remember that outfit.

"Let's go to see more of Tunapuna. You'll see them later. That's my old bicycle leaning on the breadfruit tree. I rode it to SAGS."

She showed me around her village and the river where she bathed, sometimes naked, for the fun of it. We crossed the narrowest part of the river and through a track that led us to the steep incline of St. John Road. I was tired but pretended that I was enjoying her tour. "We are going to Mount St. Benedict Church at the top of this hill."

"Great!"

As we walked slowly up the hill, Catholic seminarians sang joyfully from their dormitory perched on the hill. I stopped and listened and got the rest I needed. We reached the top of the hill, and I was ecstatic to be there at last.

"This is Mount St. Benedict, Blackboy. You don't mind me calling you that sometimes?"

"Mammy may object." We laughed.

She pointed. "See the Caroni Plains in Central Trinidad in the distance. Isn't it lovely?"

"Like you in that beautiful dress." She pretended she didn't hear me. "The Plains is a table top of greenery, and its one of the breadbaskets of this country."

"Let's go into Mount St. Benedict Church. People all over the world come here to pray. Mom came here every Wednesday to pray for her children, especially for me, and my behavior. Let's go and pray."

"You go and pray for us. I'll stay outside."

It was a short prayer. Probably she prayed for herself only because she came out in five minutes. "Do you think your mother likes me?"

"Mammy loves you very much. And what did Mom and Father say about me?"

"Mom's tongue is lethal, but so far she said nice things about you. One thing though—she said your head is like a slope. If she didn't find a fault I would have been worried. Father adores you."

We returned to Fyzabad next day, and I had my first real romance in Tunapuna.

She became pregnant. And my mother's tongue was unforgiving. "Why didn't you use rubbers?"

"I'm a big man. I didn't want to!"

Her temper raged. "You are so ungrateful! But *that no-good woman in the post office* will let you pay for your rude tongue, big man. Just imagine Joe and me got married and you never even bought a gift for us. You're cheap just as your stinking father." She used colorful adjectives for my father, and I wasn't spared.

The word "ungrateful" pained me. It became unbearable to live with my mother. I had long since apologized for forgetting to buy a gift for her and Mr. Joe. I had given them a belated gift--$35, half of my month's salary. Mammy refused it, but my stepfather accepted it, with thanks.

I passed the Civil Service examination and moved to Port of Spain to work in the Prime Minister's Office. Enid, too, was granted a transfer to the General Post Office in Port of Spain.

We planned our wedding.

My first assignment as a specialist secretary in the Prime Minister's office to cover secret investigations and conferences began on March 14, 1959. I reported to Ulric Lee, the Honorable Parliamentary Secretary. He was the Chairman of the Civil Service Re-grading Commission. The Civil Service loaned him three experts versed in the regarding of salaries.

One day before I was assigned to the Commission, I learned that the Commission's venue would be on Nelson Island, one of the Five Islands, two miles, or more, off the mainland. Enid was livid when I told her that I couldn't tell her where I'd be working, neither could I give her the assurance that I'd be returning before our wedding date.

The motor launch roared with the commissioners and me, the one-man staff, to Nelson Island. We were housed in a building that seemed fastened to rocks. I did not tell the commissioners of my intended marriage but hoped their task would finish before my wedding day.

We worked day and night. Late at nights I looked at the harbor lights and at Chaguaramas, once leased to the United States of America as a base for 99 years. I could see Carrera, an island occupied by prisoners sentenced to hard labor.

I looked at the stars and thought of my bride-to-be who was staying with her godfather because we had no money to afford an apartment. My years as a secretary/stenographer in the Civil Service were not blessed with computers or modern gadgets as a delete button. When a mistake was made on carbon paper, sometimes five between the bond paper, it had to be erased without a blotch. Accuracy made my job easy. The commissioners worked feverishly, and I transcribed my shorthand notes as quickly as possible. Whenever I asked when we would be going home, "Soon" was their answer.

The day before my wedding, I asked the friendliest of the commissioners, Carlton Bruce, "When are we going home?"

"Sunday. Why do you ask so often?"

"What time?"

"That depends on the Chairman, your shorthand, and your typing skills."

On my break time Saturday I looked at the boats that went to and from Tobago. I pelted rocks into the sea and watched their hops—tick-tack-toe. I became friendly with God again. My Sunday school teacher had told me when I misbehaved during her instructions: "Bad boys get gifts from God when they behave."

I had asked God to let the commissioners finish their work before Sunday or early Sunday morning. My Sunday school teacher was correct. God answered prayers quickly, sometimes. Later in the day the senior commissioner addressed me. "Mr. Shorthand Writer, you did well. We will be launching out Sunday."

"What time?"
"Be ready when the motor launch comes."
"When?"
"Sunday morning. What's your hurry?"
"Nothing, sir."

The good news made me see the sun's rays as I never saw it before. I was seeing the sun that Paul had told me to look at every day. Shafts of sunlight penetrated the bedroom and warmed my body.

I had a sleepless Saturday night. I got off the bed early Sunday morning, packed my things, looked into the sea and at the sun. In the distance I saw the figure of a motor launch. I felt like a leper that was going to be healed by the motorman. On Saturday night I had walked on the edge of Nelson Island and had looked at Chacachacare, "a boomerang-shaped" island, which was discovered by Christopher Columbus. There people with Hansen's disease (leprosy) once lived.

As a boy, I listened to my dramatic mother's descriptions of places, things, and people; and I did not know whether what she said about lepers was true: "Blackboy, their skins are peeled off to their bones. They have crooked fingers; their joints are turned up and down. The government sends them down to a secret island to live where nobody could see them or catch their disease."

I cringed at her stories especially when she said, "A government health officer and three policemen had gone late one night to a place where a leper was hiding. They held that leper, put him in a bag, and exported him to Leper Island."

That thought left me as Commissioner Carlton Bruce shocked me. He remembered my name. The other commissioners addressed me but never called my name. I hate people like that. (One of Enid's nephews speaks to me but never calls my name. Probably he thinks I want him to call me "Uncle." And my remedy is, if I see him first, I look away.) *They probably think I'm underprivileged.*

"Your stenography was great, Hollis Crooks. Are you a crook?" Commissioner Bruce asked.

"No, sir. When would we be going home?"

"Tomorrow."

He expected me to divulge why I was so happy to leave Nelson Island.

Two o'clock in the afternoon, Sunday, March 28, 1959, the motorman pulled up his anchor. The launch heaved hills of water. The balmy breeze cooled me all over.

The commissioners looked back at the view as the motorman sped towards Carenage jetty. Not me! I was afraid I'd be punished as Lot's wife and turned into a pillar of salt. Only yesterday God listened to my prayer and made the commissioners finish their task, and He would not want a salt man to marry that "pretty girl who worked in Fyzabad Post Office."

My 4:00 o'clock appointment consumed my thoughts. That was the time of my wedding to "the pretty girl."

Our chauffeur waited at the jetty. He graciously offered to take me to my door. I refused his hospitality and let him drop me a block away from my temporary home at Enid's godfather's residence at 1 Vidale Street, St. James. I ran down the street. Vidia Naipaul, Nobel Prize Winner for Literature, must have run down that street, too, before he left for England because he lived nearby. His sister, Kamla, taught Enid at SAGS.

Enid was in her nightgown and leaned of her godfather's iron gate. She looked into every vehicle that came down the street. She refused to get dressed and didn't fix the puckers on her gown. She remembered too well many brides were left at the altar; their grooms never came. In fact, those grooms knew in advance they were not coming, probably their mothers objected to their marriage, as my mother did. And they pleased their mothers.

She knew her parents were not coming. Father would have come, for sure, because Enid was his pet. But whatever Mom said was final. Only her sister, Versil, attended our wedding. Nobody on my side came. Enid and Mom had a big dispute few days before the wedding. I sensed, too—I could be wrong—that Mom was ashamed of Enid's big belly before marriage.

Enid saw me running down Vidale Street; it was as if she saw her savior, a willing savior. She rushed out of the gate and hugged me. Her tears watered my face. I felt the mound on her belly. It was a three-month-old fetus.

"I didn't believe you'd come because Loney didn't want you to marry me." She called my mother *Loney*. "I was standing by the gate since nine o'clock this morning, and my godfather begged me to come in. He said you'd come, but I did not believe him."

I dried her tears. "You know I wouldn't miss this day."

We rushed inside and dressed in the same bedroom.

Our only known guests, other than her sister, Versil, were Victor Skinner, her godfather, and his wife, Vida Skinner; one acted as father of the bride; the other as mother of the bridegroom. They were already dressed. It was a one-car parade and Victor sped to the church.

Enid took off the ring from her finger and gave it to me before we got into the church. It was a ring with a dust of diamond that she bought from Y. De Lima Jewelers while I was away on a "sensitive" investigation.

Reverend G.O.B Buxo, Rector of St. Agnes Anglican Church of St. James, after a short ceremony, took the band on his waist and tied my right hand to Enid's left hand, blessed us, and pronounced us, "Man and wife. You may kiss your bride." My lips barely touched hers when I kissed her.

All through the service my mind was on my mother's words when I left home: "*That* woman in the post office that you're going to marry would make you pay for your ingratitude to me and Joe. I went without bloomers to send you to school, and you wouldn't stay to help me buy a piece of board to finish build this house. You are the most ungrateful of my five children!"

Those words bled my heart of oxygen.

12

"Many of you, caregivers, will die before your patients," the Alzheimer's Association (New York Chapter) counselor said.

He looked at his audience but somehow I felt his eyes pierced mine. He behaved as if he were a voyeur who had peeped in my bedroom and saw Enid's habit of tearing toilet paper in the shape of money bills and stacking them under her pillow.

In group counseling at Brooklyn Downstate Medical Hospital Center, Dr. Andreas Adams, a Vietnam veteran, and Lorna Walcott-Brown, M.A., who headed the program, had told us to express ourselves to other fellow caregivers and that would help ease some of our stress: "Talk about your loved one's habits, the difficulties you encounter as caregivers, your family as a whole—those who help you, those who don't. Talk about your kind neighbors, even the unkind ones." Every caregiver spoke at length. I pretended that I was uninterested in being there in group therapy.

But, in fact, I was comparing my wife's behavior with other caregivers' clients. I also compared my age, and my physical appearance, with other caregivers'.

Enid was in the early stage and was stubborn as a Tobago mule that refused to pull sand out of the Courland River for commercial purposes. From my experience, of the three stages—early, middle, and late—Enid was most difficult to control in the early stage, especially her lavish spending, without accounting, and unwarranted insults to me and members of her church. In answer to an insult after a church service, I said, "Pastor Crooks, you don't have all your marbles. I have mine." I felt bad for my uncharitable remark, but I was happy that she did not hear me. Hell would have rolled had she heard.

As I listened to fellow caregivers' toils and hardships with their loved ones, Dr. Adams and Ms. Brown looked at me. They silently besieged me to release my pain. An ex-soldier said boot camp was easier than taking care of his mother. He wanted to know where he could find an inexpensive elder law attorney to advise him of handling his mother's only property—her house.

"Their fee begins at $7000," I said. "I went

to one and walked out of his office."

I saw sadness in the ex-soldier's face.

As caregivers shared their experiences, I thought of how Enid withdrew large sums of money from her savings and never paid her bills. And I could not prevent her. I knew of those withdrawals when I saw the slips in one of her hiding places, but the money could not be found. Some church members knew how to get loans from Alzheimer's Pastor Enid Crooks Lending Institution:

Tell Pastor Crooks of the love of Jesus and then ask her for a loan.

Some of those dear members were with their Pastor at a crusade in Madison Square Garden when the keynote preacher shouted into the address system, "Someone in the congregation has hidden money. Bring it up for the Lord."

Enid went into her bosom, took the permanently-stacked $100-bill from her bra, and turned it in. That was a running joke at **519** whenever I wanted a loan. Her answer was, "You are not the Lord."

Caregivers at group therapy, I remembered clearly, poured out their lament. I was mum. But I thought of how I'd found Pastor Crooks's canceled checks for a member's car insurance. I wrote him:

"Dear Brother in Christ, please pay me the money Pastor Crooks lent you to pay your car insurance. I found two canceled checks so far. The good Lord will bless you, should you repay the full amount owed to me." The religious man left the church rather than pay his debt. That Corinthian Christian, like others in her church, saw a "sick duck, with soft feathers, and plucked it."

I screened her callers after I found out some church members' intent.

"Don't pick up my calls! What the hell you knew about telephone when you lived in Fyzabad bush?"

Ms. Brown interrupted my train of thought. "Lloyd, would you like to say something? Would you like to talk about your caregiving difficulties?"

"My children should come to group therapy with me."

"Bring them," Ms. Brown said. "Dr. Adams and I would love to have them."

Dr. Adams coaxed me to continue, but I didn't.

I relived that moment, with the palms of both hands in my face, of how Trish could have lost her life:

Trish lived upstairs. She came downstairs

often in search of her mother's countless bunches of car keys. What she found, she hid. But her mother had a spare hidden elsewhere, or on her person. One Sunday morning Trish tried to take away her mother's car keys because her mother got lost more often than not, and strangers drove her home. She had asked her brother, Taariq, to drive her to church but he had come late that morning.

Enid drove out of the garage. Trish jumped by the driver's seat, held on to the door, and tried to turn off the ignition. Enid accelerated. And Trish jumped off and fell. The wheels of the Buick barely missed her. I was speechless.

An hour or more later, Enid drove into her garage. She couldn't find her church.

I didn't speak of that terrible incident. Neither did I tell that Alzheimer's patients have their own kind of accounting to aid their memory. Enid wrote down everything. She wrote: Where to meet Pastor X, whose church faces our house, with $5,000 and Pastor X's telephone number. She left that information by the phone. Fortunately, Trish had come home early from work and knocked the locked-bedroom door having heard whispers from within. Pastor X walked out. We didn't know if Pastor X had collected some sort of spoils beforehand because Enid stacked away money in places unknown. I had been lucky at times and had found enough money that paid our quarterly property taxes.

Trish followed Pastor X to the door. Pastor X didn't go into the church that *it* attended or into *its* vehicle parked down the block. *It* did so to camouflage *itself* as a stranger on the block. We had already lived on the block for twenty five years and knew Pastor X from every angle of *its* body.

Trish called Nigel, her brother, who speaks and looks like ice. His mother said he developed that personality because he was born in the Seventh Day Community Hospital's bathroom in Trinidad. She couldn't hold him any longer. She read him Pastor X's request. In five minutes Nigel came over. He lived two miles away and only visited us once in a blue moon. He walked in, said not a word, closed the bedroom door, and called Pastor X.

I pressed my ear to the door and got the gist of the iceman's ultimatum:

Pastor X, whenever you see my mother, cross the street…I'm warning you….

The next time Enid and I saw Pastor X,

Pastor X crossed the street at an inconvenient time. The traffic light was red but the Pastor dangerously walked between speeding vehicles on Flatbush Avenue.

My thoughts were back on group therapy. Caregiver after caregiver poured out their souls to the counselors. But I poured mine to myself:

Should I tell my counselors about Pierre's inhumanity?

I did not. But I thought about it:

Pierre lived in 521. We shared the dividing wall for both houses. He knew of my wife's Alzheimer's condition. He and Trish are friends, and he knew my wife as a fashion statement when she was lucid. Yet, when he saw her walking away, in pajamas, in socks, without shoes, he never brought her back inside, or made it his business to ring my bell to alert me. I missed her, and rushed outside. "Pierre! Pierre! Did you see my wife?"

"Miss Crooks went that way." He pointed at the crossroads. I used my instinct and ran in the direction of the park. She had crossed two traffic lights. I met her at the dysfunctional light on her way to Nostrand Park. I hugged her and caressed her palms as I did new lovers in my youth and brought her home.

I thought of shouting out to the counselors, telling them that Enid had walked away in the suburb of Charlotte, North Carolina, when I took a nap late one evening. She had walked a mile or more, turned right at the crossroads, and ended up in a dead-end street. Had she turned left, she would have been on one of the busiest highways in North Carolina, at dusk, walking during her "sun downing" hour. "That's their regular time to walk away. That hour is built into their brain." I learned that term in my research.

There were two letters in my pocket. I purposely walked with them to share with the counselors and the group. But I clammed up: One, written by Enid when she lived with Lloys, in a gated community in South Africa. It was addressed to her *dead* mother:

Mom, I'm kidnapped. Come with my two brothers and rescue me.

The other letter was from Lloys. It stated that she had gone to work in Johannesburg. Enid eluded her 4-year old daughter, Soley, Mozambican-born, and her nanny, and attempted to climb over the high gate:

Daddy, as soon as I got home, Soley said in Portuguese, "Mammy, Granny was running away to New York, and nanny put me on her back and ran and pulled Granny off the gate before she ran away to New York. Nanny said you'll fire her for not watching granny properly. Please, don't fire Nanny because nanny caught Granny before she reached New York."

The session ended.

"Lloyd, you haven't said much," Ms. Brown said.

"What a difference time and Alzheimer's make. Had you known my wife when she was lucid... She was a beauty."

I never returned for group therapy. And I never let church people visit Pastor Crooks. Eulah Joseph was the exception, and I love her.

Enid had a new mission when she moved into stage two. On sheets of paper Gail had written and stuck on every door: ENID CYNTHIA BAIN-CROOKS, YOU LIVE IN BROOKLYN, NEW YORK. MOM USED TO LIVE IN TUNAPUNA, TRINIDAD. MOM IS DEAD. FATHER IS DEAD, TOO. YOU HAVE TO TAKE A PLANE TO GO TO TRINIDAD. STAY HERE WITH US IN THIS HOUSE IN BROOKLYN, NEW YORK. WE LOVE YOU.

"Who is putting this stupid nonsense all

over *my* house?" She ripped off every sheet. She was as vocal and as agitated as President Ronald Reagan when he told Mr. Gorbachev to break down the Berlin Wall.

13

We have six children. Their names are Judy, Lloys, Taariq, Gail, Nigel, and Trish. Trish, the maverick, is seventeen years younger than Judy and was the only child who never lived in denial of her mother's illness.

They once formed a rival gang--the older three *versus* the younger three. Their clannish outbursts were nasty at times. Like their mother in her youth, they'd settle a dispute in the parking lot or around the dinner table. Enid and I stopped having family-get-together dinners because those dinners always ended in grudge matches: This One *versus* That One; but if a stranger attacks one of our children, he has to know he attacks all, and he'll be the victim. But their mother's condition makes them cry and mask their feelings for her (and, perhaps, if that could be their fate).

Judy hides her sadness like a school kid. She teases her mother, and she enjoys her mother's vulgarity. "Who the hell you fought today,

Enid?"

"Your mother!" Enid shouted.

"Who you cursed today?"

"Your mother mother!"

"Who else, Enid?"

"Your mother! And your mother!"

"Good girl." Judy was pleased whenever her mother reacted that way. That way was so different from when her mother prepared her a dish of grated cheese, macaroni, with dead cockroaches piled on top. Judy dumped the dinner when her mother looked away. Still Judy lived in denial of her mother's illness.

Lloys's denial of her mother's illness was worse. As much as Lloys and Enid opposed each other, and loved each other, their mantra was the same: God helps those who help themselves.

When Taariq was a sick baby, Enid took him to the doctor. But she also went to the crossroads with him and prayed to God to heal him. It was as if the crossroads had a shaman better than the doctor, and God wanted her to walk to the crossroads to show that she was making an effort to get her son healed.

Likewise, when Lloys wanted a second

child, she didn't leave it up to cohabitation with her husband. She went to the Ile de Goree, a small island off the coast of Dakar, Senegal, "where African Americans, in particular, go to pay their respect and reflect upon their ancestors' past." (I've read that quote in a book that Lloys had lent me.) She felt that her ancestors would intervene for the good. Her daughter, Soley, was born after her visit to Ile de Goree. "Daddy, your belief is your belief," she said, when I held Soley in my arms for the first time in Mozambique.

When Lloys was three years old, she had annoyed her mother. "You're ugly!" her mother said. "That's why the babysitter had to drunken you to sleep."

As much as Lloys loves her mother, and, to me, they are one chip off the same block, I suspect Lloys has not forgiven her mother for that gaff. I hope I'm wrong.

Their pull and tug was eternal.

"Lloys, I'll lock you out if you come in *my* house after 8:00 o'clock tomorrow."

"Mammy, this is summer. Eight o'clock is daylight. We are not in Trinidad and Tobago."

"Is that so?" Their conversation ended.

Lloys waltzed in at nine the next day, and

the door was locked. She slept at a friend's house that night, and many months after. Mother and daughter's feud over when the curfew hour should begin and end never fizzled in Lloys's teenaged summers. At times when I had bravely intervened, Enid said, "You are just her father. Stay out of this." But the nights she had locked out Lloys she cried till morning. I pretended I didn't hear her.

In South Africa Lloys took her mother to a doctor who diagnosed: *Enid Crooks is suffering from Alzheimer's disease.*

Despite the doctor's diagnosis, Lloys lived in denial of her mother's illness for many years. Her e-mail reads:

Daddy, I believe mother is resting her mind. We must believe that she will DECIDE if and when she's ready to return to lucidity as we know it. I haven't written her off. I can relate to her TIREDNESS (emphasis added).

On leave from her United Nations post in South Africa, she became the primary caregiver when she *relieved* me for a week. Three times in that week Enid walked away only to be brought back home by Good Samaritans and New York's finest—our policemen. Lloys treated her mother as a normal person: She refused to lock the doors because she equated her mother's Alzheimer's disease with *TIREDNESS*.

Lloys always guarded her parents and felt we were equals with anybody no matter who that person was — a president, a king or queen. In Mozambique, she had introduced me to the crème de la crème and *felt* that I kowtowed to those people because I took too many photographs of them. She walked away from her company and spoke in my ear. "Daddy, why are you so star struck? My mother would never behave like you. She never kowtowed to anybody!" She walked off as if she said, "You are so nice, daddy," with a stern look.

My photography ended. The pictures I took were never developed.

At 14 years old, Taariq praised me for something I did and excluded his mother in his praise.

Enid showed him who is worthy of praise. "Taariq, your father loved you so much that he went to see a football game instead of coming to see you, his first son, in the hospital, on the day you were born. For that matter, I didn't see him until two weeks after Judy was born. Continue to praise him and *not* me."

Taariq had saved his meager allowance (ten cents weekly, which had just been increased to one dollar a month) and bought a set of knives for his mother's forty-first-birthday's gift. He thought his knives would have been received as if they were pyramids brought to her backyard, and she'd use the knives to protect the mummies, and for her other domestic duties. His mother thought differently. She threw the knives at him: "You bought them to kill me!"

I never said it before, but her comments to Taariq worried me. *Has she serious mental problems under cover?* Now I look at the way he cradles her in his arms to and from the doctor's office and into his car. He had cried the day he saw her coming out of the bathroom with her pamper at her ankles. "How could this be, mammy? How could this be?" His tears flowed freely.

I always laugh at this encounter: "Mammy, you told me that you and my father have nothing to do with each other, so how come you're pregnant?"

"You are fourteen, and you're telling me that I have a man with your father?" She slapped him.

"No, mammy."

"Then, what do you mean?"

He did not answer. He never sassed back

to her again.

Taariq wished he could turn back the hands of the clock to when she hunted him in Nostrand Park. When his friends saw her, they shouted, "Snake, she is coming." He would drop the basketball and run as fast as he could. She had warned him, "Keep away from that drug hole." He knew she would flog him in front of his friends for disobeying her.

Nigel visited us rarely. When he did, he planted a kiss on her forehead the way her father did to her. That delayed kiss hypnotized her. After he left, she asked: "Did Nigel give you the money he owes me?"

"How much he owes you, Fats?"

"That's not your business."

"Then how would I know how much to collect from him?"

"You didn't collect any money, so why bother."

Whatever he did after the two detectives "hellish trial of my son," as she called it, she forgave him. Her thumb of equal kindness for her children was always on Nigel's part of the scale.

Their sideshows were plentiful. She had called him to wash dishes and noticed a ring on his finger. "Nigel, you are wearing a ring on your wedding finger. Are you married?"

"Yes, mammy."

"When?"

"Yesterday."

"Where?"

"Downtown."

"And you didn't invite me?"

He bowed his head.

"And you, a married man, are still living in my house?"

Then she questioned me. "You, Hollis! You knew Nigel got married yesterday?"

"All I knew was: He was sleeping in the basement. A woman called him. I woke him. He answered the phone, and he left."

"Was he dressed?"

"I did not know when he left."

Their syrup overflowed for each other, as I expected. I left them in the kitchen and went to bed.

Trish was born in the bicentennial year of America. She is a graft of "the possible" and "the impossible." She's is as gifted as a never-caught thief, and, like Mr. Never-Caught, should have been chosen by the Bush Administration to settle the dispute in the Middle East. She would have put *possible deals* and *not impossible deals* in the same sweaty hat and would have told the Palestinians and the Israelis, "Anyone could choose first."

She applied that method on me when she was eight years old and wanted an increase in her allowance. She had put two pieces of paper in my hat. One had $1 written on it, the other $2. "Anyone of us can choose first, daddy." She never lost a bet. Whatever dollar amount I chose, that was her increased allowance. Then she developed a new way of frightening us for an increased allowance: "Daddy and mammy, if you all don't increase my allowance, I will run away and join a gang." I used to be very afraid that she would run away if we did not accede to her request, but her mother never batted an eyelid. "Leave whenever you are ready, Trish," her mother answered. "That's one mouth less to feed."

For her entrance examination to be put in first grade in New Vista Private School, she couldn't spell the word *dog*. She sneaked out of the examination room for my assistance, and I repeated how to spell *d-o-g*. When New Vistas sent us Trish's spelling test result, one word was wrongly spelled: *G-o-d* for *d-o-g*. Enid was elated and called Trish by her pet name. "Bookey, it's better to know how to spell *God* than any stinking *dog*. God made you pass the test for New Vistas."

Gail, nicknamed *Snapshot,* from date of birth, documented her mother's love in her essay. She loved drama from the day she was born. The midwife had put her mother on the delivery table. Gail pushed herself out of her mother's passage and fell on the floor. The confused midwife snatched her up, and said, "Lord, I hope the matron didn't get a *snapshot* of this delivery." That delivery was in Port of Spain Colonial Hospital, and Enid was too weak to make a ruckus with the midwife for letting her new born fall out of her. Knowing my wife, had she the strength, she would have put that midwife over hot coal for that mishap.

On Gail's assignment for a Master's degree in Social Work at Columbia University, Professor Sormanti asked students to write an essay of their choice. Gail's essay is titled *A Mother's Love*.

"*Mommy, where are you going?*" Gail begins her essay.

"*I'm going home. If I don't go, Mom will beat me,*" Enid replied.

"*Mom is dead.*"

"Mom is not dead! She's waiting for me with a whip."

"You didn't call Mom's friend 'ugly Carmen' or pushed down the Indian woman by the stand pipe to get water before her, so Mom has nothing to beat you for today."

The once independent business woman, mathematician, community leader, pastor, no longer exudes those definitive characteristics.

Twelve years ago Dr. Sundar diagnosed my mother having Alzheimer's disease, a form of dementia which is "a loss or impairment of mental power." Enid Cynthia Bain-Crooks, my mother, was the epitome of "mental power."

I envisioned we would travel the world after her retirement, and I'd lay my problems at her feet. I'd ask her advice on how to make my marriage work as hers.

She was my syntax police in grade school, and I could never trick her with money. She multiplied by three figures, calculated the taxes, and knew how much change from whatever amount of money she handed the cashier. As she walked into Korean stores, the Korean language was spoken instead of English. The men at the fish market said, "Here comes the math woman;

watch your fractions to the penny."

She was scornful. Our father cleaned our feces as children. Her nickname at Con Edison was "Spit Flies." She told her supervisor at an office party, "You can't talk over the food that I have to eat because spit flies." My mother felt her supervisor harassed her unduly because she rebuked her table manners. My father disagreed, in my mother's absence, of course. He cited the Alzheimer's experts: Enid's "increasing impairment in carrying out executive functions" is probably the true cause of her supervisor's harassment.

I feel cheated of her love because I can no longer accomplish the things I longed to do with her. We traveled to several countries in Africa; and she, once cleaner than an unused bar of soap, had to be monitored for her hygiene. I was the mother, and she, the child. Once she had an opinion about everything, mine never mattered. Now I have to coax her to speak. She was always elegantly dressed. Her avocation was Pastor of Divine Truth Assembly and dressmaker for her children. Her sister, Sylvie, a professional designer, taught her. I was a fussy teenager, but I loved the clothes mommy made for me.

On our last stroll, I took her to the linen

store to choose drapes for my bathroom. She did not like any of the sets, had little or nothing to say, and I had to rely on my questionable taste.

My father bowed to her over-powering aggressiveness, a trait seen in my siblings. Our fire and drive to conquer the world are also mommy's trademarks. Equally impressive was her ability to laugh at anything as her father, who died from Alzheimer's disease. She sang "O Perfect Love" at my first wedding anniversary, and I cried because I sensed that was the last time I'd be hearing her beautiful voice. She switched from soprano to alto. Now there is no delicious laughter at home, once the liveliest house on East 26th Street, also called **519**.

My moods traverse into depression. I wonder what would happen to my mother if my father could no longer take care of her. He takes care of mommy the same way he took care of me as a child. My siblings said, "You are daddy's favorite." I felt mommy was. He never complains about his caregiving duties, and I think he should be closely watched. Of course, I could just be making a big deal out of my pain and life's disappointments of things gone awry due to mommy's health. Nonetheless, I spend valuable time with my parents. I look at their wedding picture on the wall. Then I look at them, clandestinely, and compare the way they looked then and now. I could see, sadly, the effect of Alzheimer's on one and the effect of caregiving on the other.

On the train, or in the company of friends, I find myself fighting back tears at the thought of her, and if her fate would be mine. I have come to the conclusion that I should just live each day to the fullest with no thought of tomorrow. Maybe I should skydive or parachute out of an airplane with President Herbert Walker Bush in his next attempt. Such scintillating thoughts are short-lived because I quickly revert to my hidden sadness. Alzheimer's, you are Mr. Go-between. You are destructive to Mommy.

Writing "A Mother's Love" and at the same time looking at the protagonist having dinner, she, not knowing if she's eating steak or snails, makes me distrustful of helpers. From childhood she would rather starve than eat chicken. She said chickens are nasty because they go in the canals and eat the worms. I hit the roof when a trusted caregiver gave my tactless mother stewed chicken and boasted, "I got Enid to eat chicken." The reason why I didn't knock that bitch to the *floor was because Purdue chickens are grown in broilers in America; they don't eat the worms behind my grandmother's house in Trinidad. Still, at times, in mommy's left-over feistiness, she'd say, "I don't eat what you are putting in my plate," irrespective of the fact that she doesn't know what's in her plate.*

Her stories about Friday fights in grade school are classics. I possess bits of my mother's wit and sharp tongue. When my tongue got me in trouble, I worried about my faux pas, but mommy stood by what she said, no matter the cost.

Her illness has taught me to take nothing for granted. My mantra to my clients is: Each moment in life is precious. Although I validate my clients' feelings, I always reveal their strength, partly because of my training in social work, but largely because of the appreciation and understanding I now have from dealing with my mother's illness.

I had accompanied a friend to a hospice to see her relative. I was only interested in driving my friend's new car. I didn't know what hospice meant, and my unconcern for the people in the hospice was major. I now have total empathy for clients coping with illness-related issues. I advise them where resources and services in the community are, and how to go about acquiring benefits. I've learned not to internalize my clients' problems. Internalizing my mother's illness impaired my judgment in the past.

Caring for the sick is an 'honorable social act.' I see my mother's love in the affectionate, wordless gestures that Alzheimer's disease cannot control.

14

President Chissano visited us in the summer of 1998. He gave us two sculptures by Reinata Sadimba, "one of the most important artists of the entire African Continent." One sculpture is a woman nursing herself from her breast; the other is a woman with many children forging out of her body. The President told us the significance of those terra cotta pieces.

Before the President's arrival, a secret service individual checked our block, our basement, all the rooms in our house, the backyard, the alleyway, and questioned me about the tenant upstairs.

"Why was that man asking you all those stupid questions?"

"Because President Chissano is coming here, and the United States Government wants to make sure that he's safe when he comes here to have lunch with us."

"The Government thinks we'll eat him for

lunch."

President Chissano arrived about eleven in the morning. The security people and uniformed policemen remained in their cars, but the President's personal bodyguard came in with him, and I could see that he mentally appraised the condition of the room where we sat. He remembered Enid and me for he had accompanied us with his President on three trips in Mozambique.

The President leaned over me and said softly, "Maseve Lloyd, how is your wife? Did the meditation exercise help?"

In Mozambique, we had stayed at his and Lady Chissano's pleasure at Casa Redonda, a mansion surrounded with cascading blooms of bougainvillea of every hue. Their redolence perfumed us. The mansion overlooks a tributary into the Indian Ocean and is guarded by soldiers in clean khaki uniform. He had sent a transcendental meditation guru to the mansion to help Enid with her memory problem in whatever way he could.

"Let's start now," the guru said. "These meditation exercises will help our memory. Before we meditate, Mrs. Crooks, you must make up your own password. You alone must know it. You must say that same password to yourself every day of our meditation. Do you understand?"

"Yes."

"Are you ready to begin?"

"Yes."

"You said the password to yourself?"

"What password?"

"The one I just told you to make up and say to yourself."

His questions and her answers went back and forth. Then he assumed that she had a password. I smiled.

Our exercise began.

He squatted on the floor. I can't remember what else he did, before or after his chanting, but we followed his movements and instructions. Enid squatted for a while and followed his instructions half-heartedly.

On the second day, it was the same rigmarole: "You remember your password, Mrs. Crooks?"

"What password?"

We began. The guru looked at me as if to say *I know she doesn't remember her password.* Nonetheless, he began his transcendental meditation exercises.

Poor guru. You haven't seen anything yet.

Wait till tomorrow.

Tomorrow came, and Enid held court. She was the stand-up comedienne. She refused to squat. The guru and I squatted on the floor with unburdening laughter. He never came back. I often wondered if he had told the President the truth: that he should not be paid for Mrs. Crooks's sessions.

Since the guru had stopped coming, we took that free time to sightsee. Daily we walked through the track that led to the ocean. An Australian tourist engaged me one morning as he walked gingerly behind us. "Do you know if there are land mines here? Before coming to Mozambique I was warned about land mines."

"For three weeks, my wife and I had been walking through this track."

"So there are no land mines here?"

"My wife and I are still in one piece." He and I smiled.

The next day I hurried her off the breakfast table. "Fats, let's go by the ocean early because President Chissano and his wife invited us for dinner." As we reached the spot where the Australian tourist questioned me yesterday, she turned back. "Quirks of memory" of the land-mines discussion reminded her of danger. But yesterday she couldn't remember her password. That is what bothers me about the zigzag ways of her disease.

All the occurrences that took place in Mozambique left my mind when Lloys brought her mother back from the President's fifty-ninth birthday party that was held in Upstate New York. I did not go because I was afraid of Enid's unexpected tantrums.

"Daddy, my mother had a nice time." All our children put "my" before *Mother* or *Daddy.* She left for her hotel in Manhattan.

"You look lovely, Fats. How was the birthday party? Did you dance with the President?"

"I want you to leave my house now!" she said.

"What's wrong with you? The President gave you too much alcohol?" She's a teetotaler.

"Leave my house now!"

"Just like that. I'm asking you about the party, and you are putting me out. It is *our* house."

"You heard me? Leave now."

I contacted an old friend. To hide her identity, I call her Nancy. For four years after my retirement in 1992, I had taught her and three other adults to read. I taught them the look-and-say system. One morning my friend did not take out her homework. "Lloyd," she glowed, "can I read something for you?"

Nancy read the first letter she had written in 61 years. Her letter thanked me for teaching her to read. I pretended something was in my eyes, but I was really drying a stream. She ended, "If you ever need help, a shelter, or anything, I'm here."

I thought Enid would have forgotten that she had told me to leave *her* house. But every day she ranted, "Leave *my* house!" I could no longer live with her swansong. But I was happy to leave. I was a very tired caregiver and welcomed her dismissal. It is a shame how people hide their true feelings.

I summoned our six children to a meeting on our plastic-covered chairs. It seldom happened that all of them were in Brooklyn at the same time. They gathered in the living room. I got completely brain dead when I saw them. I never wanted such a day to come. Better said, I never wanted such a day to *occur in my life.* In a way, I was afraid of my children's opinion, probably afraid of them more than their opinions. Parents who say, "I don't care a hoot about my children's opinions" are full of baloney, and sausage, too. Seeing them was like "funding my own critical studies."

Taariq had told me before that incident, "I only come to this house to see my mother. Nobody else!"

Nigel had said, "The next time I come to settle a complaint about you talking down to my mother, I'd set an example."

I looked at him, and he said, "With you!"

Their mother's Alzheimer's disease affected their reasoning, too. They couldn't decipher the untruth of their mother's made-up stories about me who *dutifully slaved behind her*. Anything she said about me was the gospel to them. They should have gone to hear her gospel at Divine Truth Assembly. Her church was empty because of her gospel.

I sat on my favorite chair and did not look in their faces. I went straight to the subject. "Your mother told me to leave *her* house, and I'm leaving."

"You long wanted to go, so go. No big deal!" Nigel's outburst wasn't new.

I did not make a ceremony about what had happened with their mother and me, but my meeting with them reminded me what my mother had said when I left her house with a huff and a puff: "Children can eat their parents. Parents can't eat their children."

Our children, except Taariq, found an excuse why they couldn't keep their mother: They spoke of their obligations to their own families. Taariq said, "If my father goes, I'll move in with my mother no matter what it costs."

Lloys said, finally, "I have to go back to Mozambique, but Khafra will come and stay with my mother when his boarding school is on break."

No one was at home when I left my voice mail number on the table.

That first night in Nancy's basement was another painful night in my life. The feeling was similar to when mammy had her third child and she could not afford to keep me. She had taken me to live with my godmother. Mammy dropped me off, and drove away in the TGR bus. That moment is forever vivid in memory.

Up to that time, Enid and I had lived together for 39 years. We had quarreled and cursed each other in our frustrations. We didn't sleep in the same room for many nights; but we went to bed in the same house.

On my second day of bachelorhood, I checked my messages on pay phones. It was

Enid's voice: "Hollis, where are you? When are you coming home? I can't sleep. I'm waiting for you."

Every day my mailbox was full: Only Enid's messages were recorded as she cried for me.

I called Milly. "I'm free to visit you any time."

"Free from what?"

She laughed, and laughed. The automatic operator spoke. "Your time is up…Drop in a dime." I did.

"Why are you laughing, Milly?"

"You're going back home, for sure, maybe tomorrow. You love your wife more than you'd want to admit. You needed a holiday away from caregiving. Your children should know you're sick from your wife's sickness. You boasted of them as being really smart. If they are smart, they should pay for a vacation for you, and get a temporary caregiver for their mother until you cool off."

"Can I come by you?"

"For what?" Her voice came over the pay booth as if she were in front of me. I felt her scorn.

"You can drop by for pots and pans for cooking, but you really don't need them because you'll be going back to your wife by the weekend."

On my second month away from home, I

checked my voice mail, and I heard Taariq's voice. "Daddy, I'll be moving in with my mother. She can't stay there alone. Khafra is there with her, but he'll soon be going back to South Africa to go to school."

It was midsummer, and I felt claustrophobic in Nancy's basement. My basement at **519** is spacious. When the children were small they lived there. There are three bedrooms, a living room, a laundry room, a bathroom. There was also a fridge with jugs of water. Our children drank the sodas before they got cold. They only came upstairs to eat or show me their homework when I didn't go downstairs. When *Roots* was a miniseries, they hardly came upstairs.

There was also a television in the basement, and I had warned them that it should not be put on during weekdays. "Leave the boob tube alone, except on Friday nights after you do your homework."

What child could stay in a basement and not watch the shows that their friends talked about? I knew that no normal child would obey me. I didn't always obey my stepfather and mother but told my children, "When parents speak, a child is supposed to obey them, *always*." So when I left the rule that nobody should put on the television during the week, I knew that was a "big joke" that came from me, once a disobedient boy, now a parent.

In Trinidad I went to see *Bonanza* in a man's yard. He put his television outside for the villagers to enjoy their shows. If he had charged me a quarter for each show, he would have had a nice bank account.

What I customarily did as I walked downstairs in **519** was to touch the television to see if it was warm. If it was warm, I would make a big fuss and threaten doomsday. Nigel, about seven then, didn't know my bluff. He heard my footsteps, ran for a jug of ice water, threw it on the television, and the box exploded.

Fats rushed downstairs. "You could've killed my child because of your stinking rules."

I intuited she knew our children broke my no-televison-during-the-school-week rule regularly.

Memories of **519** haunted me in my friend's basement. I bought a keyboard that helped my loneliness. The more I played *The Nearness of You*, the song that brought Fats and me togothor, and *For All We Know*, the last song that Johnny Nash sang in his Trinidad and Tobago concert, the more my tears flowed.

Then a thought overpowered me: *How could I not know that Alzheimer's disease affects the patient and the caregiver in different ways? It wasn't Fats that chased me away.* It was her Alzheimer's disease — that brain thief.

I remained in Nancy's basement for another week: I was not ready to resume a caregiver's duty. It is a *very difficult* duty. It wore me down. It frustrated me beyond bounds. Sometimes the worst thoughts came to mind--sinful projections that I won't say; but didn't mind if other people said it, and it came true. Every time such a feeling crossed my mind, I prayed about it.

"Milly, I'm calling you to let you know that I'll be going back home at the end of the week."

"That's not news. I thought you were already there, Lloyd. "

"There's no need for your sarcasm."

Just the thought of going back home revitalized me. I was ready to resume caregiving duties. The time away from home was therapy.

As I opened the front door of **519**, Fats screamed. She ran to me. I dropped my keyboard and embraced her. She had lost about fifteen pounds. I lifted her up and kissed her endlessly. I was happy to be back to my home, sweet home, and to be back with my loving wife.

Khafra returned to South Africa.

"Are you hungry, Fats?"

"You come home early to cook for me?"

"Sure."

I concocted a recipe from things in the kitchen cupboard: beans, salmon in a tin. Corn meal and flour turned to dumplings. She didn't skip a beat with her compliments.

"Boy, poverty in Fyzabad bush taught you how to cook stones without spice and make it taste good." Her appetite was enormous. Her compliments made me feel as if I'd never left **519**.

"Is that the genius of Alzheimer's disease?" She didn't have the sense to know that I left her for two months, but she could resurrect jokes about my childhood poverty without losing a beat?

Oh how I love her. A new kind of sweet love for my wife began in earnest. And I vowed to myself that I'd never leave her again.

15

The sun stung us. Its heat on our bodies was from the glare off the eastern windows in the living room. Mary James braved the heat. She was in her backyard and supervised the gardener who mulched the earth and molded perennials. Felicita Raynor and her son, Myles, chatted in Jamaican patois. Then he switched from patois to American English in a nano-minute and answered a phone call.

Gwendolyn Clarke, our tenant on the second floor, was silent. In fact, I couldn't tell whether or not she was there most times. I knew her whereabouts when she left a stone on the step to let me know she's upstairs, and that I could call on her for help, if needed. She taught me how to collapse the wheelchair to make it more accessible to take Enid out of it and put her in bed. That knowhow helped tremendously. She was a home health aide at Precious Blood Monastery run by Catholic Charity for aged nuns, and she is familiar with the habits of Alzheimer's patients. Whenever I was melancholy, she said, "Praise God that your wife is still eating. When she stops eating that's when you should get worried and know that she's going down."

I had just finished cutting Enid's hair and had dressed her in shorts. She was restless but I didn't give her *Risperdal* to keep her calm. Eyes closed, effortlessly, I hummed, a medley. From age 50 I'd forgotten every song I knew and mixed one song with the other. Whenever I played the piano I found myself playing a medley: two lines from many tunes. And I'd smile remembering, if Enid were fully lucid, her words would have been: "You mean up to now you can't play a tune right."

She dug into my side. "You know what Mr. F did to me?" She called his full name, and no part of his name denotes *F*.

"He was your parents' best friend when you were a little girl."

"You want to hear what he did?"

"No."

She elbowed me like Jersey "Joe" Walcott did his opponents in the boxing ring. He and Joe Louis were my favorite boxers. But I'm still disappointed with Joe Louis' aloofness. Not Enid.

He had come to Trinidad and Tobago and had remained atop Queens Park Hotel and waved to his fans. I thought he would have come down to shake our hands like Paul Robeson did. At Robeson's concert in Globe Theatre, he opened the doors and let poor people in after the bigshots paid.

    A noise was heard at the fence that separated Mary from Felicitia.

    "Fats, Mary and Felicita are at it again."

    She did not answer.

    We changed our seats and hid from the sun's rays. The leaves of the giant hackberry rustled on our roof. It is of the regenerative genus and trimming its branches was a waste of time because they grew back quickly. Mary only trimmed the branches over her house. There were loud quarrels between Enid and Mary about who should cut the hanging branches completely off our house.

    In summer Enid had loved the hackberry for its lofty shade to her guests at barbecue parties. But in autumn she no longer loved the tree when it shed leaves and the clutters in the leaf axils were dropped into our guttering and when leaves dirty our backyard which is tedious to clean.

Mary's reason for not cutting the tree was, "I met the tree there when I bought the property."

I paid a tree cutter $600 to cut the branch over our house and cart it away, and that temporarily ended the quarrel between Mary and Enid. Those branches have regenerated, but Enid is none the wiser because of her sickness.

The quarrel between Felicita and Mary raged. Probably the sun's rays affected them, too. Many years ago Enid had said, "Their never-ending quarrels were because each wanted to boast of having the best looking house on the block."

"Everything I do me monkey does do. That is why I put up this wall," Felicita told a passerby when she complained about Mary, the monkey.

The solid brick wall in Felicitia's porch completely blocked Mary's northern view of Brooklyn. After twenty plus years of complaints by Mary—Mary and Felicita have died—New York City Housing and Preservation Department is yet to come write a violation or okay the wall that separates their porches.

From our living room I listened to the two neighbors, but Enid was noncommittal. "Fats, listen. Mary just called Felicita a Jamaican devil."

She elbowed me again. She didn't want to

hear about Mary and Felicita. "You want to hear what Mr. F did?"

"How old were you then? How old are you now?"

I knew she couldn't tell the answers. But I looked for miracles. She did not know that I am her husband. But she knew I was related to her in some special way even though she did not trust me at nights. Whenever she was distrustful, I'd say, *Fats, Fats,* and somehow the throw of my voice bred familiarity.

"Fats, tell me what Mr. F did." I asked the question to prevent her elbow from goring me.

She took a roundabout route to tell a story. That became a new style to talk of the past. She began. "Mom didn't know that I walked out of Osmond's High School and went to St. Augustine's Girls' until the time came to pay school fees."

"Those were great times then, compared to now." I doubted she understood the difference between *then* and *now*.

She began a biography into her secret past as if her rite of passage was to elect me as her therapist. I didn't look into her eyes for fear that I might be mistaken for a stranger whom she distrusted. Children of our generation in Trinidad and Tobago were considered "very rude" if we stared our parents when they scolded us or even spoke to us. Looking into our parents' eyes meant we were challenging their authority. Looking into Enid's eyes in that stage of her illness—learned from studying her old and new habits—meant threatening her. Instead, I looked at the floor and did not grasp the import of her words until she said, "Mr. F locked the door and made me take off my clothes."

She spoke of his abuse during her pre-teen years, and the more she spoke, the more relaxed she became. She was clear as my Christmas mouth organ without spit. Her words dripped and fragmented. They came out as if she had drained all out of her memory. And what remained was her body next to mine. And even her body didn't make sense now because no part of it ever revealed those things before.

I didn't want to hear more of the noun, *Mr. F,* and the verb, *did*. She said a complete sentence but I blanked out words and made her precise thought a fragment. Yet I couldn't escape the subject, *Mr. F,* and its verb, *did*.

I approximated the age of this little girl at that time. Then I wished I were deaf. I also wished she had kept that secret to her grave. It wasn't my wife speaking. It was Alzheimer's disease, the hacker. It was the "brain thief" that broke into her cranial computer and divulged her secrets. If, before that release, I only loved my wife because she is the mother of our six children, Alzheimer's made me *fall in love with her, and forever.*

I am no longer that "hypocrite in early marriage" who said empty words when asked about my relationship with my wife: *Good enough.* I now say, "Fats is my wife and my lover."

Felicita and Mary's bandying died to a whisper, and Dwayne Arbuckle's sweet-pan music was heard. He played *Jesu Joy of Man's Desiring.* His pan shone, and his touch with two ping pong sticks (sticks with rubber tips) was beautiful. It was a welcome change. He healed my sadness at that moment. He stood on the sidewalk in front of Mary's house and played his pan solo in memory of his brother, Donovan Arbuckle. Donovan, an ex-serviceman, 35 years old, had shot himself July 14, 2003, on the very spot that Dwayne stood.

Enid's warm legs touched me, and I took her into the bedroom where I forgot the sadness of that morning.

Night came. I showered her. She pointed at a bottle. She no longer knew the word *perfume.*

I perfumed her, showed her the bed, and made motions of the easiest way to climb into it. Each night she took different routes to get into her bed, but she always reverted to the way I taught her. She made a sign for me to come to bed. I obeyed. I hugged her wounded body, and as she slept I thought what would happen to her if I'm not around at the last stage of Alzheimer's.

Fate had ceded her illness to my care. Taking care of the chink in her womanhood was letting in light to my darkness.

I couldn't think of anything humorous about her to combat my feelings. On that warm night the words of the Alzheimer's Association counselor came to mind: "Many of you, caregivers, will die before your patients."

At midnight I stopped the intake of solids and liquids. At nine in the morning, Dr. Avidah Rudberg, Diplomate of the American Board of Urology, was scheduled to operate on my prostate for the first time. Even though he had said a week beforehand, "Lloyd, it's a simple operation," throughout the night I had thought: *If I die, who'd take care of Fats the way I do.*

16

Caregivers forget their cares when their Alzheimer's patients evoke latent comedy from within them. Enid sent me reeling with one liners, some as clever as Chris Rock's political commentary, others as caustic as Joan Rivers' when she knifed the fat off Elizabeth Taylor, no longer trim and beautiful.

Cousin Ann became my secondary caregiver and brought comedy back to **519**. I was ecstatic when she said she'd sleep in. Enid knew her for many years, and that was a plus. My children were happy with Ann's decision because with Ann around their help would be needed less. They never expressed that thought. I did.

Ann packed her things neatly in drawers in the middle bedroom. Her father and my mother, both deceased, were brother and sister. We reminisced about our parents' lives and their oral tradition passed on to us.

I told Ann her duties, advised her on

medication, and added, "If you have time read *The 36-Hour Day, A Family Guide for Persons with Alzheimer Disease, Related Dementing Illnesses, and Memory Loss in Later Life.* That book would help you in understanding Enid's behavior." I pointed to the book in the library.

Enid was asleep.

I warned Ann of Enid's moods on mornings.

"You are exaggerating, Hollis. We are two Christian women. We would be singing hymns for the whole day."

"Ann, when you are telling Enid to do something, please, *do not* look directly into her eyes. She'd think you are challenging her in her house."

Ann dismissed me as if I spoke nonsense.

"Cousin Ann, please answer all phone calls. If people call and introduce themselves as *pastors who want to speak with Pastor Crooks*, hang up."

"Why?"

"Because they maybe calling to borrow money."

"Don't they know Enid has Alzheimer's?"

"They know."

"I'm a Christian, and if I find any money Enid hid in any corner of this house, I'd give it to you when you come."

"And you'd have 10 percent of whatever the amount is. That's a deal."

I left for Central Park and sang on my way to the subway.

Give me the streets, and you give me heaven

Give me city buses, and you give me freedom

Give me the iron snake burrowing through the boroughs

Give me Central Park as my spoils. And I'd beg no more.

Detrained, in Manhattan, I ordered Chinese takeout, walked through Central Park and nibbled my meat. Artists beckoned to me to have my portrait sketched, but I didn't oblige. I rolled on the grass and winked at a sunbather with a sun screen about to cover her face. She winked back, and I said, "You still won't have my color." "Who said I want your color?" She laughed aloud. I laughed louder. New Yorkers have the best one-liners.

The park was filled with lovers, families, and groups. They frolicked with gaiety. Tourists from Fifth Avenue to Columbus Circle waited on buggies and Pedi cabs for tours of Manhattan and inhaled the smell of horse manure. I had a wonderful day and the iron snake took me back to my favorite borough—sweet Brooklyn.

Ann met me as I turned the key. Tears flooded her eyes.

"What's wrong? Did something happen to Fats?"

She sobbed uncontrollably.

I rushed inside. Enid was studying the *Brooklyn Community Board 17* letter sent to her three years ago. She was on the first page. She had long forgotten how to read. She looked normal, unscathed, except that she was still in her nightgown.

Ann stood with her packed clothes bag in hand. I coaxed her not to leave.

"What's wrong, Cousin?"

Enid darted at me. "You brought that woman to work domestic in my house, and she doesn't even have a high school diploma!"

That was an original for an Alzheimer's patient, I guess. Caregivers have told me of classics, too. But I held my laughter. "Fats, why didn't you let Cousin Ann bathe you?"

"Bathe me? She's not my cousin. I'm no lesbian!"

I was caught between a cousin whom I thought would be taking the load off my feet and a wife possessed with tantrums.

Ann found her voice. "Cousin Hollis, that book you gave me to read doesn't have any advice on how to handle Enid. I needed *The Forty Days and Forty Nights Book of Jesus in the Wilderness*."

I rushed to the bathroom, emptied my bladder which showed greater signs of my prostate problem, laughed aloud, and rushed back outside to face the comediennes.

"Cousin Hollis, I'm leaving. I'll send someone with a car for my things."

"Cousin Ann, come in the kitchen with me," I said softly. I opened the fridge, poked my head inside, dismissive of the cold vapor that cooled my sweat. "Cousin Ann, please stay until the weekend."

"Enid is the worst person I've worked for."

"When she curses you, curse her too. Forget that you are a good, Christian woman."

"All right."

My advice worked. They cursed each other frequently. I didn't care because they didn't fight. Ann worked with us until she got a better job.

Ann had cleaned her drawer when I was in

Tobago for my father's 90th birthday. In the bottom of her drawer, wrapped in toilet paper, neatly folded, was $400. Enid had told me, in confidence, "I'm going to hide everything from your thieving cousin because she cannot be trusted in my house with my money."

Ann had ignored my promise that if she had found any money she should keep it, give it to me personally, and I'd give her 10 percent. She gave the $400 to one of my children who never turned in the spoils.

17

Trish handled her mother's tantrums best. This could be because she was our last child; she had lived longest with us, and had seen her mother through all the stages of AD. Enid had given her a nightgown as a gift. But whenever Trish put on that nightgown Enid fought for it. Sometimes I was afraid they would hurt each other.

On Sunday, May 3, 2001, Trish got married. When she drafted her wedding program, she showed it to her siblings and me. Her mother's name was omitted from the program. I was annoyed, but Judy was furious.

"You're getting married in the church your mother founded, and her name is omitted from your wedding program. Why?" I asked.

"Daddy, you know why." Trish was blunt. "I don't want my mother to do something …" She changed the word she was about to say. "I don't want mammy to say something that's not on the program."

"If your mother's name is not on your wedding program, we would not be coming."

To appease me, her wedding program, minutely altered, read: *Mother and Father of the Bride would light a candle.*

Bishop Wesley Wiley and Apostle Patricia Wiley officiated, and Trish-Ellen Crooks became the wife of Curtis Wayne Jackson, Jr.

Judy bitched with Taariq. "Trish had the nerve to leave *my* mother out of the wedding program and only let *my* mother light up a stinking candle. Could you imagine that, Taariq?"

Taariq doesn't trust even his shadow in his sleep, and he didn't trust the answer he should give to his favorite sister's question, so he became mum.

In the reception hall Judy exchanged her altered program with the Master of Ceremony's original program. The program went on, as the one in my hand, until the M.C. said, "Pastor Enid Crooks, mother of the bride, would bless the food."

I looked at my program and instinctively looked at the bride who sat at the bridal table. Her face revealed: *What the hell is going on! I didn't put my mother's name on the program to bless the food!*

Pastor Crooks sat by my side. She didn't know that *her* name was called.

I held her hand and took her to the dais. Before the M.C. handed her the microphone, I whispered, "Fats, when he gives you the mike, bless the food. That's all you have to do." I repeated, "Just bless the food only. Don't say anything else."

A quick glance at the bride's disgust reminded me of nuggets of her character. At seventeen, she was a teen counselor at Brooklyn Downstate Medical Hospital. She enjoyed my discomfort when she advised me on safe sex. "Daddy, try these condoms. Or do you want the edible kind?"

Trish was never afraid of her parents as her older siblings.

Her mother had told her that I wanted her aborted, which was true. Conversely, her mother wanted Judy aborted because she thought I would not have married her.

My mind went back to the past. I compared Trish, the bride, about to see her mother bless the food *with* Trish, the seven-year-old child, who probably prevented her mother from committing a felony. When her mother drove her to the Seventh Day Adventist School, a knife fell out of her mother's purse. She begged her mother, "Don't kill Annette today, mammy. Please, don't kill the supervisor who wants to fire you."

Now Trish, the bride, was about to see her mother again in action.

"Pastor Enid Crooks would bless the food," the M.C. repeated.

Pastor Crooks began: "Curtis, you married Trish today, but don't beat her because I would come and get you. I mind Trish from small. I sent her to college. I educated her. She's no dunce. I'm warning you, Curtis. Don't touch her unless you are making love to her. Love is all we need." She had said that last line in many of her sermons, and now it was in her "quirk of memory."

Judy ran out of the reception hall knowing that she had deliberately doctored the MC's reception program, and had put her mother to bless the food. Judy also knew when her mother held the mike her mother would not stop in a minute. I refused to look at the "angry" bride because I had forced her to put her mother's name on the program. I felt, more than ever, that I was still living in denial of my wife's sickness.

Pastor Crooks was in the *cul-de-sac* of her thoughts, and her thoughts were stuck on Curtis.

The first time I had heard the word *cul-de-sac*, I did not know its meaning. I was the specialist stenographer on a Commission of Inquiry appointed by the Prime Minister of Trinidad and Tobago to investigate the soldiers' behavior. Soldiers had invaded Carenage village, almost on the western tip of Trinidad; Chaguaramas was on the western tip, and it was the soldiers' base. Said base was once occupied by American soldiers during World War II.

Carenage villagers heckled and provoked the soldiers, the new kids on the block. They were accustomed to the policemen only. "Those soldiers think they are better than the police who guarded us for so many years." Some villagers threw stones at the soldiers' trucks when they came in and out of their base.

The soldiers retaliated unexpectedly.

Trucks of soldiers unloaded themselves onto Carenage and beat every villager in sight.

At the Inquiry, a Commissioner asked a young soldier, "Where were you when this melee was going on?"

"*At* the *cul-de-sac.*"

I did not know what that word meant. But from reading back my shorthand notes of the evidence of soldiers who preceded him, I realized the word meant "a street closed at one end."

Similarly, Pastor Crooks was at the *cul-de-sac* of her thought when she blessed the food. The name of her closed street was Curtis, and it was a dead end street.

"Curtis, my husband is a coward, but I am not. I will come and fight you for my child. I'm not afraid of you and all your family...."

I assumed the MC enjoyed bacchanalian feasts in the past. He could have taken away the microphone from Pastor Crooks in a nice way, but he let her go on and on. An idiotic smile pasted his face. I later debated the MC's performance with Gail who said "the MC's approach was the right approach. No one could predict what *my* mother would have done had he taken away the mike from *my* mother at that time."

I rushed to the dais, got my wife, and walked her gingerly to her seat. Her dress fitted her beautifully. I would never have guessed the cost of that dress if I didn't find the bill. (Had I asked, "Fats, why pay all that money for a dress?" Her answer would have been, "It's my money!")

"You like how I blessed the food, Hollis?"

"It was great, Fats!" I squeezed her hand. That was our code of approval.

The MC reverted to the original program, and he called on the designated Pastor to bless the food.

Later in the evening, I eased myself up to the bridegroom. "Curtis, please accept my apology for my wife's behavior. Tell your people in New York and those who came from South Carolina to accept my apology, too."

"That was fun, Mr. Crooks. We enjoyed it." He hugged me. And we laughed aloud.

*   *   *   *

She was in the middle stage of AD, but she was still preaching.

The song service had begun. I played the piano and her voice was above the congregation's. Then her voice was not heard. I played all the hymns on the program and repeated them.

Lord, where is Pastor Crooks? Where the hell did she go?

I got off the piano. I looked at the program, changed the Order of Service, and addressed the congregation.

"Good morning to you all. It is so nice to be in the Lord's House today. Pastor Crooks will soon be back. Let us go to Testimony Time. We are not following the program today. Get up and let me hear how God has been good to you. He has been good to me, always. He gave me a good wife, seven lovely children, and a job. I was fired from my last Wall Street job, but God gave me a better job with entrances on 48 and 52 Wall Street. He gave me a job that gave me a bonus every year, free meals, car service when I worked overtime, and other benefits. He even gave me a job by the East River. It is not the River Jordan. But it is a river."

"Amen. Hallelujah!" the congregation echoed.

Five people were the congregation. The bulk of members had stopped coming. Four were complete strangers. It seemed all of them came looking for a church to pour out their sorrows and speak of glad tidings. The first woman prayed. She testified. She prayed. She testified. Four of them did the same. My role as interim pastor must have lasted an hour or more. When the last person testified about the goodness of God, Pastor Crooks walked in. *Where was she, Lord?*

I struck up her signature hymn in E flat, *I Must Have the Savior with Me*. She sang aloud. Her voice was a beautiful ribbon on tone. Her gospel that day wasn't a blooper.

After church, as I entered the house, Trish shouted, "Daddy, mammy came home and looked for you, and I told her you were in church. Did she find the church? Did she come back with you?"

"She's parking her Buick."

Enid's sickness developed, and many Sundays she couldn't find her church. One Sunday she was completely lost after church. Eulah Joseph was in the car with her pastor and thought her pastor took another route because she was going on an errand. Suddenly, she stopped her car. She picked up a stranger who demanded money to show her the way home. Eulah, a soft-spoken woman, tactfully talked the hustler out of money and out of the car.

One night a man drove Enid home. He told me she was at the gas station. She told him that she had a headache, and if he could drive her home. I thanked him and offered him money.

"No, sir. I know the sickness. My mother had Alzheimer's. Take good care of her."

"I thank you very much, sir." I barely lifted

my voice. Tears had the better of me.

He patted my shoulder and said, "Take care of yourself."

A similar incident took place when she stopped driving. I took her to the Brooklyn Labor Day Carnival to sell my novel, *Grenada Ghost*. She stood next to me but she disappeared when the mammoth crowd in a carnival band surged by at the intersection of Eastern Parkway and Franklin Avenue. The carnival parade ended at six in the evening, and I stood at that same spot until long after midnight. A young man, about nineteen years old, brought her to me. He told me he walked the length and breadth of Eastern Parkway and looked for me. "Your wife asked me to find you." He, too, refused money for his help. I hugged my wife and hid my tears. *Brooklyn, New York has good people — very good people, I can vouch for that in stone.*

18

Gail's caregiving on Saturday was routine for a time. As she walked in, I walked out.

I roamed the theater district. My free time gave me a new kind of life. I eavesdropped on theatergoers who discussed Broadway shows. I stumbled on tourists who admired New York City's neon lights. I joined jaywalkers and blocked yellow cabs that had the green light. I answered that hustler's question one more time.

"Brudder, you hava dollar? Trying to get home."

"Me no speaky English, brother"

The hustler melted into the landscape when he spotted a policeman on the beat. He showed me his dirty-finger sign, and I pushed mine higher.

The silent beggar was my next stop. He sat on a stool on 42nd Street, between Sixth Avenue and Broadway. He had his money cup (sometimes a brown-paper bag) in front of him and his sign read: INSULT ME AND PAY ME. I put one dollar in his cup, called him "a lazy son of a bitch, %%%," walked over to Eight Avenue peepholes, and ended up in Colony Music Center at 49 and Broadway. Going through the racks of music at Colony consumed my time, and I settled for Sinatra's *Nothing But The Best*.

I went back to the beggar's station. He smiled as I approached. His smile melted me. I did not curse him. We trash talked with each other, and I gave him four quarters.

Then I rushed back to Brooklyn and relieved Gail.

The phone rang.

"Mr. Crooks, is Pastor Crooks there?" Pastor Crooks was the caller's counselor before she moved to Virginia.

"Verna, Pastor Crooks has Alzheimer's," I whispered.

"Send Pastor to spend two weeks with me." Verna's voice pitched in the cordless phone. "Mr. Crooks, I'll take Pastor Crooks everywhere with me. We'll have a great time."

"Great, Verna. You are a godsend."

Judy bought her mother new clothes. I called Verna and reminded her of Pastor Crooks's Alzheimer's condition. I must have told Verna no less than five times how tricky is an Alzheimer's patient—"the patient and the disease."

"Verna, you must *always* take charge of Pastor Crooks's luggage."

"Yes, Mr. Crooks."

"On the flight to you, the flight attendants would be in charge of her luggage, and she would be pushed out in a wheelchair. When she's coming back, impress on the desk clerk that Pastor Crooks must be put in a wheelchair because she has Alzheimer's. In fact, the wheelchair information is on the computer."

"Don't bother. Everything will be taken care of."

Enid reached Virginia without a hitch. With the good news, I showered and left for my favorite place in the world—New York, New York.

Verna took Enid to Mississippi. From Virginia she left Enid in charge of her luggage.

I spent the day in Manhattan at all my haunts. The silent beggar's sign looked bolder: INSULT ME AND PAY ME. I put a quarter in his cup and cursed him until my throat parched. Twenty yards away was another beggar. His cardboard sign close to his chest, said, I NEED MONEY TO BUY

WEED. I entered the subway to downtown with a broad smile.

There's no better school of learning for psychiatrists, psychologists, philanthropists, and out-of-towners than New York subway. At Atlantic Avenue, a woman pushed herself between the straphangers with her wet umbrella and wet clothes. It seemed her umbrella didn't help in the pouring rain. A beggar toured the cars and began his elegy as the train rocked: "I don't do drugs. I don't do alcohol. I can't get a job. I'm asking anyone who'd be so kind to give me a penny, a dime, a quarter, something to eat."

The woman handed him her wet umbrella.

"Lady, what the f--- I'll do with that wet umbrella?"

"You're begging. It has value. Rain is falling, so sell it."

Their exchange was psychology 101. A straphanger passed his stop, purposely, to hear the dialogue between the beggar and the woman with the wet umbrella.

I was still laughing when I got home. I didn't care to pick up the phone because I expected no calls. My lovely wife was in Old Miss, and no call was important. I reluctantly picked up the phone.

Verna's voiced pitched. "Mr. Crooks, Mr. Crooks, thank God you're home!"

"Is anything wrong with Pastor Crooks?"

"She lost her luggage!"

"All? All!"

"Yes."

"Didn't I tell you to *always* take care of her luggage?"

"Pastor Crooks looked so normal. She talked as my old pastor. She counseled me over and over about how to take care of my boys. I didn't see why I had to keep an eye on her luggage because I thought she would have thought I'm treating her as a silly child. The way she counseled me on the bus when we were going to Mississippi....."

I cut her off. I didn't want to hear more of that nonsense. "What should I do now, Verna?"

"Can you wire *her* money?"

"Why not *you,* instead of her?"

"That makes better sense, Mr. Crooks."

The New York-Virginia-Mississippi-New York round trip was a graph with high and low points.

Verna confirmed that Pastor Crooks was landing 4:00 p.m. on American Airline at Kennedy. I thanked her for giving Pastor Crooks a wonderful outing. Like an overly protective parent, I made sure and reconfirmed the flight number and time of arrival at Kennedy. I also reminded Verna that Pastor Crooks is booked with wheelchair service.

Judy drove to the airport. We reached Kennedy at 3:00 p.m. and read the arrivals and departures on the monitor. AA from Virginia arrived on time. I sent Enid with wheelchair service to Virginia and expected her to be pushed out. All the passengers came off the flight from Virginia. A woman in a wheelchair was pushed by an airline employee. I rushed to her. She was not my wife.

Judy was parked outside and hoped I'd soon be out with her mother. She rushed inside and called out, and I told her that her mother had not come on AA. She rushed and parked her vehicle in the parking lot.

Half an hour later, Enid could not be found. I called Verna. She answered. "Pastor Crooks left on the confirmed flight, on time."

"With wheelchair service?"

She stuttered, and I hung up on her. I didn't want to hear *any more nonsense about Pastor Crooks looked normal and talked normal at the airport counter and she counseled me....*

Judy came from the parking lot and didn't see me with her mother. She panics over

Ice and Eyes in the Sun 263

everything. She didn't this time. As the automatic door opened, she pushed her head in and asked a customs officer if there were people in there who came in from Virginia. "That flight came in on time long ago."

"Wait here, daddy, in this area where people come out of Customs." She rushed off to search for her mother.

At 7:00 P.M. she came with her mother.

"Where was Fats for the past three hours?" I asked.

"Daddy, I met her walking about in British Airways waiting room. Don't ask me how she got there."

Fats and I had our usual fun talk at bedtime. "Fats, you came in late from Virginia? Why?" I handed her a cup of hot cocoa.

"That driver was crawling on the road. I hate slow drivers."

"Me, too, Fats."

"You are a liar! You always say slow down when I'm driving fast."

*   *   *   *

We returned from Downtown Brooklyn shopping and were one traffic light away from our home. We traveled on that route for thirty years. At the intersection of Foster and Flatbush Avenues, one short block from our house, the traffic light was red. She stopped. The green light came on, and I thought she didn't see it. I nudged her, "Fats, move. We have the green light."

"I'll bet you the money in my bosom that you don't know if I should turn right or left?"

"Cars are backing up behind you. Move!"

She didn't budge. "Hollis, you don't want to win the $100 in my bra?"

A Jamaican dollar-van driver honked his horn. His cap peak faced northwest. His bumper touched hers. "Bitch, move!" As he shouted his curse in patois, I remembered Friday, December 3, 1993, when a passenger of a-dollar van shot and killed the driver in front of our house. All the passengers burst into our living room, and knocked Enid to the floor, as they scampered for safety. The police eventually came inside our house to investigate and Enid shook like a leaf in their presence.

Drivers honked their horns on Flatbush Avenue. The Jamaican cursed louder. "Blood clot $%&#$@%...."

I realized Enid completely lost her memory.

As the light turned green again, I did not tell her that she had to *turn east* because I knew she was utterly confused. I pointed my left hand and let it do the talking.

"This way, Fats," I said calmly. Winning the hundred-dollar bill permanently stacked in her bosom wasn't my motive; getting away from the dirty tongue of the dollar-van driver was. And at that moment her mental dictionary had no pages of the cardinal points of Brooklyn. I held my breath until she drove into the garage.

Wanting to discuss the day's events, I called Milly and told her what had happened at the traffic light. She was stern, yet she watched her words, not wanting to make the mistake of letting her tongue loose.

"Why are you still living in denial, Lloyd H. Crooks?" I felt her disgust of my stupidity. "Don't you think it is time you take charge of your sick wife and stop being afraid of her and what she thinks about her cars, her property, and her church? Take away her blasted car keys!" She was about to continue her advice but stopped abruptly.

I kept silent. Then she continued.

"What if your wife and her car kill an innocent child running home from school to show his parents his school report card?" Her anger came through.

Two weeks later I gave her 1991 Buick, with less than 25,000 miles on the odometer, to charity. Hidden in the glove compartment were spare keys.

Nighttime brought fresh peace to me, and I was thankful for Milly's friendship and advice.

Within three months Fats had deteriorated a great deal. I gathered her toiletries after I showered her. She pointed at a bottle, and I said, "That's perfume, pretty girl. Now let us listen to the news."

On every channel was Osama bin Laden's long, bearded face.

A *Fox* news announcer said, "No one knows of bin Laden's whereabouts."

"How you can't find him and he's on your own TV, fool!" she shouted.

19

I packed my luggage for London on the news of my brother-in-law's death. Then I focused on what should I do with Fats. I called Lloys in South Africa.

"Daddy, my mother can stay with me during your stay in London. Book a wheelchair for her."

I booked her on South African Airlines, October 6, 2002, and booked myself on Virgin Airlines to London on October 7.

My new worry was whether Enid and Lloys, chips off a controversial block, would agree. Alzheimer's sharpened Enid's sarcasms, and Lloys was no willing receptacle for her mother's insults. Neither calmed the storm with soft words: A spade was not a shovel, and a thief was not a pilferer. Whoever was angered called a spade *a stinking spade*, and a thief *a big thief*. The adjectives were loftier most times. After their quarrels there was unconditional love between them.

SAA's departure was 6:30 P.M.

At 4:30 we were at JFK.

How could I be sending my sick wife to South Africa by herself after all these restrictions at Kennedy Airport after 9/11?

My guilt subsided, prematurely, when I handed the guard at the airport's fortress Dr. Sundar and Dr. Valasareddi's letters that stated *Enid Crooks has Alzheimer's disease...She should be accompanied to the airline counter by her husband.*

"Who is traveling?" the guard asked. His bouncer tone was massive.

"My wife is, but I would like to accompany her to the airline desk because she has Alzheimer's disease, and she would not be able to find her way by herself." I saw his mood, and I meant to be extremely polite. "Sir, these are letters from her doctors."

"I don't want to see them."

First, it struck me that he, as I, still had the pungent smell of burnt bodies at the World Trade Towers in his nostril. For that, he should be extremely cautious in checking my wife's document, I thought. Then I concluded he was carrying out administrative duties to the letter of the law, plus his law of impertinence to senior citizens.

I opened the doctors' letters and appealed to him.

"I don't want to see them! Only she can go in."

"Please, call your supervisor."

"You can look for him and find him."

My body blocked the traffic queued between cordoned ropes. I appealed to him, but he didn't budge.

I stepped aside, spoke to my wife in a brave tone, but I wept within.

"Fats, I put a Dagwood sandwich in the bag for you to eat on the plane if you get hungry. Hold your suitcase in this hand, and don't take off your purse from around your neck until you get to the airline counter. Let the lady at the counter take out your airline ticket, and she'll put you in a wheelchair and have someone take you to the plane. I have money in your purse for Mincing. You know who Mincing is?"

"You think I'm stupid? Mincing is Lloys. You gave your children all those stupid nicknames."

My fear of her getting lost in the crowd was gone. I was drunk with happiness when she revealed "quirks of memory."

I pinned the large scarf around her shoulder and fixed the collar on her dress. I purposely put her in bright colors for easy discernment.

She moved off at 4:45 P.M. She meandered through the ropes. I knew at that moment that I would not leave the airport until I counted every plane in Kennedy's sky.

Fats looked as a disguised hobo about to ride on the wing of the plane with a bag around her neck, another pulled, and a scarf that motioned like a wobble pump that the pilot may borrow to supply fuel to the engine.

On the ramp, I looked all around me like a pickpocket who was learning the escape routes before he grabbed a tourist's purse.

At 5:15 p.m. I changed my gaze and compared the sunset at Kennedy Airport with the sunset that touched the tarmac at Mozambique Airport. The sun looked bigger in Mozambique. Then I saw a familiar figure that blocked JFK's sunset. I knew that dress with a scarf that came up the ramp.

I'm dreaming? No.

"Fats?"

"Yes."

There was no use questioning her. Alzheimer's, with its brain problem, was the answer. I presumed: She got confused in the body traffic of airport travelers who followed the cordoned ropes;

she didn't remember why she was among so many strangers, and the best thing was to find her way home. When she had eluded me on a Staten Island ferry, she had no money but she found her way home. I wondered then if she had jumped the turnstile. Worse still, what would have happened if she were caught? Late from work one night, I didn't jump the turnstile, but a policeman in hiding made me pay a second token. He said he didn't hear the noise from the turnstile and what he'd do if I didn't pay. Luckily, I had another token otherwise I would have had to walk from downtown Manhattan to Brooklyn late that night.

On many occasions when she eluded me, she found her way home. Once I screamed at a Livery cab driver who stopped for her. Finally, I found a temporary solution: I held her hand firmly wherever we went, even in the men's room. Anybody who wanted to interview me had to accept her as my bodyguard. She became my two-in-one. But still my new safety measures for guarding her were not foolproof. She continued to walk away at times.

As planes ascended, I looked at my watch and hoped she'd catch her flight. She was disheveled but her accoutrements were intact.

I rushed to the cordoned ropes. Another guard was now at the helm, and I spoke hurriedly, "My wife has Alzheimer's disease. She went in before and got lost. Her sickness causes confusion in her brain. Could you, please, let me, or someone, take her to the airline counter and see that she gets a wheelchair for her flight to South Africa?"

This one, too, is not listening to me.

I realized that that guard was adept at multitasking. He directed traffic through those cordoned ropes, spoke to many people, but I interrupted him constantly as the line got longer.

"I have letters from my wife's doctors. She's going to South Africa and someone has to take her to the desk. She is running late. She had all her malaria shots. Please, look at these papers."

That new guard never looked up or down to see if I were Long John Silver or if an eye were in the middle of my forehead. But a passenger heard my cry. "I'll help her." He helped Fats with her luggage.

"Thank you. Thank you. Thank you, Sir." I raced to the ramp, overwhelmed with joy. That relief was life given to me anew: I deem it similar to when the bandit took the nozzle of his gun off my nostril, and I wet myself. The bandit asked for the nugget ring on my finger. It was very tight, and I had to use my teeth to get off the ring. When I looked at mug-shots of criminals in Brooklyn's 67th Precinct, I didn't think of the bandit's crime, but of his honor: He kept his promise. He had said, "I'll spare your life if you didn't look at my face." I obeyed.

    The kindness of that stranger in the airport and that of the bandit's will never be forgotten—one helped my sick wife who meant the world to me to find her way to the airline counter; the other did not pull the trigger, and I'm alive to take care of wife until the day I die.

    I resumed my position on the ramp and counted airplanes in Kennedy's sky to 10:00 P.M. Enid's flight left at 6.30 P.M., on time.

    Sleeping pill *5421* coaxed me to sleep. The phone rang next morning, and I snatched it.

    "Daddy, South African Airlines allowed me to board the plane and take off my mother. I met her eating a big sandwich. Stay in London as long as you want. Convey my sympathy to Aunt Cynthia. Cheer up, daddy."

    She felt the tremor in my voice.

"Tell Fats next time we'd be traveling together to London to see Aunt Cynthia." I smiled. I remembered how Fats had described my sister. In the summer of 2004, she and I traveled to North Carolina to spend two weeks with Trish. At Newark Airport, a female passenger fetched her out of the bathroom for me. We almost lost our flight because the censor buzzed her. Two female guards took me into a closed room to witness her intimate body search. The censor traced a penny hidden on her person. I suspected she picked up that penny in the ladies' bathroom.

On our return flight, the complications were just as discomforting. I had to leave our luggage with strangers to find a bathroom for her. When she got in the bathroom she had difficulty to take off her clothes and do the needful, as usual, and I listened to the women as they grumbled aloud: "What the hell is she doing in there?...Is she making rope?" Their comments itched to answer them. But it was an itch I dare not scratch.

That was the last time she flew or traveled out of Brooklyn.

20

Charmaine interrupted me while I was writing this true love story. I thought she was reminding me to buy pampers for Fats as she did each Friday.

"Mr. Crooks, I'm sorry to disturb you."

"That's all right, Charmaine."

"Today is my last day with you."

I was shocked.

Charmaine was a capable secondary caregiver. She had worked for us for two years. She knew that my wife was losing her ability to speak, and she encouraged her to make conversations. I knew the hours of the day without looking at a clock. At 10:00 o'clock she switched for Maury Povich's pregnancy test--"Who's the baby's father." But she was most vocal when Jerry Springer came on at 11:00 a.m., and Jerry's fans heralded, "Jerry! Jerry! Jerry!"

"Miss Crooks, that sinner man is on again with all those loose women fighting over a man and exposing their parts on the TV. I don't know why government allows a show like that on TV."

The following day, and all the days that followed, I knew it was 11:00 a.m.

"Miss Crooks, that dirty-man Jerry is on again. He has a man on who left his pretty wife to live with a hairy man."

Jerry Springer came to mind before I asked a question. "Why are you leaving us, Charmaine? Has Miss Crooks been nasty to you?"

"Miss Crooks is a nice lady. I know how to handle her. I had cases like her before."

"You got a better job?"

"No. The doctor says my baby is in a bad position, and I need to rest."

"What baby?"

"I'm eight months pregnant."

"What! Where are you carrying that baby?"

"People asked me that same question when I had my first baby."

"If Miss Crooks could have expressed herself, she would have thanked you for helping her. I thank you for both of us and hope everything goes well with your pregnancy."

I thought of when Enid and I were young and she had said, "Hollis, I didn't see *it* this month, and it is *your* fault."

"Why didn't you take your damn pills, Fats?"

"You know those damn pills don't always work."

"Because you forgot to take them daily!"

"Why are you barking at me? You could have used condoms instead of me swallowing these damn pills. Why don't you swallow some for me?"

"After this fifth baby is born, we'll be having no more sex."

* * * *

I fired our next helper. She had worked for two weeks.

"Judith, did you give Mrs. Crooks her meds today?" I asked politely.

"You are the worst person I ever worked for. You ask me the same stupid question everyday as if I'm a fool."

"My wife is taking *Neurontin* that prevents her from getting seizure, and if she gets another seizure and ends up in the hospital, her doctor will ask me when she got her last dose of *Neurontin*."

"Let her doctor call me!"

"Mrs. Crooks is my wife! And if you had a medical degree, you wouldn't be here."

"I know that."

"I don't even have your phone number." I fired her; but I really liked her.

Myra was next. She came with accredited testimonials. She was sixty years old, clean, soft-spoken, and recommended by a past member of Divine Truth Assembly. "Brother Crooks, Myra is a good church woman. Employ her. She does a lot of things for her church. She worked with Alzheimer's people before."

I employed Myra and told her that we had a guest staying with us.

Janet Williams was our guest from Trinidad. She was 64 years old, blind, and beautiful, with a swagger. She weighed about 300 pounds or more. We had last seen each other fifty years ago. At fourteen she was chubby and cute. When I was seven years old, my duty was to rock her to sleep. Her parents and mine lived as family.

From the first night of her stay she showed her independence. "Hollis, all I want you to do for me is to show me how to find the bathroom. Tell Myra she doesn't have to take care of me. Buy a box of cornflakes—the original flavor—and leave it with a bottle of water by the bed before you leave on mornings. I am on a diet."

I smiled.

"Why did you smile about my weight?"

"How come you know that I smiled?"

"Blind people have hidden eyes."

At five every morning Janet showered. Her stealth was shattered when her stick lifted the phone off the cradle and the phone buzzed and woke us. Enid observed everything about Janet that morning and after.

I was locked out when I collected a package from the postman. The wind blew the door in. The bell was not working. I shouted for Enid but Janet answered. She knew Enid's inability to understand instructions. She had that cinematic way about her from childhood, and I knew she would find a way to let me in. And she did in a jiffy. My only house rule to her was that she should not drop paper on the floor because Enid would stuff it in the toaster and push the lever down. She did that before and caused a mini fire ball.

Janet was a bondswoman before she lost her eyesight. She knew all the court marshals and bailiffs and tipped them handsomely to keep her abreast of prisoners' movements. So I knew I could depend on her skills.

Enid couldn't speak but she wanted to be in Janet's good graces. Somehow I felt she was jealous of the attention I gave Janet. She watched how Janet navigated her way with her stick and meant to be of service to her. Janet woke up at five, and Enid was up, too. She held Janet's hand, led her to the bathroom, waited at the door until Janet came out, and led Janet back to the bedroom.

"Fats, go to the bathroom now and brush your teeth," I said.

She went into the kitchen instead. I couldn't understand how she found the bathroom for Janet but not for herself.

Every day Enid tiptoed and peeped at Janet in the bedroom to see what she did.

Janet had perfect hearing. "Fat, Fats, is that you? Are you looking for me?"

Enid tiptoed out of the room, but did not answer. The word "Yes" was still in her vocabulary and "Let me tell you something" was her pet sentence. But when I asked, "What do you want to tell me, Fats?" she couldn't say.

Janet was hip to Enid's limited vocabulary

and her hide-and-seek game to broker friendship. It became Enid's way of befriending the stranger. When Janet smelled Enid's perfume, she said, "Fats, I know you are there looking at me." Enid tiptoed out the room and laughed.

Enid shocked me when she went on the bed and fell asleep next to Janet. She finally trusted Janet as a friend and not as a stranger.

Myra was never late for work. I left on my gallivanting trip as soon as she walked in. Janet's bondswoman's keenness was forever in motion. She made mental notes of Enid's disposition before and after Myra came in.

"Myra, where's Enid?"

"She's somewhere in the house. She's not lost."

Janet called me when she returned to Trinidad. "Hollis, Myra is not attentive to your wife. She doesn't care about you either. She told me that she doesn't like to work for black people. "

"Why?"

"She said that she vacuumed the house on Monday and you wanted her to vacuum on Thursday, too. She said she vacuums her house once a week and she doesn't see how any black man, accustomed to nothing, could get her to vacuum his house twice a week."

"It's only two small rooms she has to vacuum, and it is because of the traffic in those two rooms. You know how small the rooms are."

"I'm blind, but I can see that Myra is not the right woman to take care of Fats. She pretends she's a caring person when you are home. Hollis, try and come early one day when she doesn't expect you, and you'll catch that f****** bitch watching TV, and don't even know where Fats is."

I ignored Janet's complaint. Myra was a "good church lady" based on recommendations. My observation proved Janet to be a good person. Nonetheless, I came home early one day, as Janet had advised. I had given Myra a birthday gift the day before. In addition, she worked two hours, and I gave her a day's pay. She usually leaves at six. At four, I came home to relieve her.

"Where's Mrs. Crooks?"

"She is inside sleeping."

"You looked at her?"

"Yes." She didn't miss a TV byte.

"You can leave now. Thank you, Myra."

I packed away the groceries in my hand. Then I walked into the bedroom. I screamed so loud that my neighbor, Mary James, heard.

Enid's neck was stuck between the bed and the wall. If she had shifted her weight on one side I didn't know what could have happened. I pulled the bed forward and relieved the pressure on her neck. I lifted her head back on the bed, slowly eased her body straight, and I examined her neck. When I lifted her out of the bed jam, I asked her to turn her neck.

"Are you okay, Fats?"

"Yes." The fact was she didn't know the difference between *yes* and *no.*

"Is your neck hurting you?"

She touched it.

I pressed my hand on her neck. "You're okay?"

"Okay."

"Is your neck hurting you?"

"Okay."

I did not take her to the doctor. Instead, I reverted to mammy's holistic remedies and treated my wife to a warm bath. As a boy, whatever hurt me--a scorpion, a dog, a fall from a tree when I stole people's fruits, a pulled muscle--mammy bathed me in warm water, touched the aching spot gently, dried me, gave me a gulp of butter, and greased me thoroughly. To this day, I don't eat butter, and I hate oily dishes, or oil on my skin.

Throughout the night I monitored her. She snored louder than ever.

Myra came in the following morning, and I told her of the way I met my wife. She made no comment. I told her again, and she said not a word.

When she left for home that evening, I called my friends for their views:

"June, you have helped me out many times. But had I told you that after you left work I found my wife's neck stuck between the bed and the wall, what would be your reaction, especially if I came home and met you watching TV?"

"I'd say, Mr. Crooks, I'm extremely sorry to hear that. Is Mrs. Crooks okay? Did you take her to the doctor?"

I called Angela and posed the same question.

"Knowing your wife has Alzheimer's, I should have checked on her more often. I'm awfully sorry to hear the way you found your wife after I left."

"Georgia."

"I hope you are not letting that woman come back to take care of your wife? She doesn't like to work for black people so you don't need her anyhow."

"Janet."

"Are you with that f****** woman, Hollis?"

"Hell no!"

"I knew Myra is a bitch. When I was there I saw the change in your wife's behavior as soon as she walked in. Not even water I let that woman give me when I was thirsty. I didn't tell you how I felt, but I knew you'd find out for yourself."

I asked every friend's opinion. But I didn't tell my children because I was afraid they would have told Nigel. His mother was off limits for people like Myra. Judy had told him, "Tom is harassing me on the job."

"What he looks like?" Nigel asked casually.

She described Tom.

"He's the only Tom on your job?"

"Yes," Judy answered and thought that matter was closed.

A week passed.

As Tom stepped off the company's premises onto the sidewalk, Nigel appeared from nowhere, called the name, *Tom*, and Tom answered. Nigel snatched him, lifted him into the air like light weights in YMCA gym, and he walked a block with Tom suspended in air. People probably thought they were part of the Barnum and Bailey circus on Third Avenue, New York.

In the middle of the second block Nigel said, "The next time you provoke my sister, I'll drop your %&%$& body on the concrete, nigger."

I did not want Myra to be lifted out of his mother's house in any form or fashion, so my children were told of Myra's attitude long after the incident.

On the bed I prostrated and thought my wife could have choked to death. My thoughts raced "from the sublime to the ridiculous." Then my thoughts raced to my trial before a jury. It was as if I were a court reporter again in Trinidad and Tobago writing in Pitman's shorthand the judge's summation to the jury. This time, I was imagining my trial: The People *versus* Lloyd Hollis Crooks.

My mind roamed forever. At the age of seventeen years, lawyers came to R.N.M. Donaldson, the principal of Oxford Commercial College, and hired me to take down the judge's summation in shorthand. After translation to English, I got a big salary of ten dollars from Barrister Misir and other lawyers.

My mind would not stop roaming: Myra in the box giving evidence: "When I left Mrs. Crooks she was fine. I left as soon as Mr. Crooks came in. I checked her before I left work. And Mr. Crooks even told me, 'Thank you, Myra.'" Up to that point, Myra spoke the truth. I couldn't deny that.

Daylight met me still thinking of how it is so hard to prove one's innocence at times. As a child I had lied on Mr. Wheeler, and he couldn't prove his innocence. My mother had washed his clothes for a month, and she sent me to collect one dollar. Mr. Wheeler gave me the money, and I lost it. My mother depended on that dollar to feed her children, pay her rent of one shilling (twenty four cents), and for other pressing needs. My mother cursed Mr. Wheeler. She believed me, not him. He couldn't prove that I was the liar.

How could a jury tell who was the liar if Enid Cynthia Crooks had broken her neck and had died? I might have been the accused.

Eleven o'clock took long to come that morning.

I showered Fats, dressed her, and made breakfast. I put the dishes in the sink and waited on eleven o'clock.

My mind continued roaming. *Probably God got Janet and me together again after fifty years for a reason.*

Myra rang the bell. The grandfather's clock chimed eleven.

I rushed and opened the door. She was beautifully dressed. Her short-cropped hair smelled of the shampoo she used. Her perfume moved with her. She wore a white cotton top, Capri shorts, and flat shoes. She rested her bag on her favorite television chair. She walked to the kitchen sink to wash the dirty dishes.

"Don't wash them, Myra."

She stared at me. Staring at me as if I should never tell her what to do was her habit. "Why?"

"We thank you for your past service. Here's an extra week's pay."

She dragged the envelope from my hand. Her glare penetrated me afresh.

She picked up her purse and walked out.

I found words to describe her after she left: Nasty, nasty words.

21

I dressed Enid for our afternoon stroll. Mary James opened our gate, hugged, and kissed her. "Girlfriend, your husband is taking you to Nostrand Park?"

She smiled.

"Mr. Crooks, how are you getting on?"

"Am putting one foot in front and one foot behind and counting on God's mercy."

"Me, too. But my arthritis is killing me."

Felicita Raynor stopped watering her plants. "Mr. Crooks, God will bless you for not hiding your wife in the house. My friend was sick with that same disease, and her husband didn't take her anywhere because he was ashamed of her. She died last year. What's today's date, Mr. Crooks?"

"October 4, 2005."

The day was as hot as mid-July. We sat on our favorite park bench where we had watched Trish, five years old, climb on the monkey bar and then chase pigeons that flew from trees to the ground for bread crumbs. Those same pigeons or their offspring waited on the regular-park-bench inhabitants for food. Enid, in lucidity, had named them "the parkies." The parkies fed their pigeons. Then they threw bread crumbs by our bench and the pigeons flocked around Enid and me. The pigeons seemed angry as we refused to move.

"Why are you doing that, Miss? Didn't you hear of bird flu?" I asked.

"How much you'd pay for this?" The woman parkie pointed to her middle passage.

I was ashamed of her behavior but said nothing to her or her team. It was on occasions like those that I knew Enid was sick with a disease that restricted her speech and strength. I also realized that she was "the one who had the balls." In Enid's heyday that parkie would have known the true smell of her feminine middle passage on that hot day.

We walked out of the park, and she pulled me in the opposite direction. I knew the reason for that tug. She wanted to visit her friend, Marion Scanterbury. Marion was in her wheelchair. She had been ill for a long time. Enid put her hand into Marion's and left it for no more than ten seconds. She released Marion's and held mine to show me that she was ready to go home. That was the last time the two institutions saw each other. Marion died soon thereafter.

On the crowded B8 bus, I rushed for a seat for her. The woman I deprived from getting the seat said, "He rushed for a seat for that thing." She made other uncharitable remarks that irked me.

At our stop, I held Enid's hand as the kneeling bus made it comfortable for us to step off. I wiped my wife's dribbling nostrils with a paper towel. The driver closed the door, and a woman shouted, "Let me off here. Let me off here, too, driver."

She ran up to us. "I'm sorry. I did not know your wife is sick. This is not my bus stop, but I came off to apologize to her for what I said."

"My wife cannot speak. But we don't need your apology."

This is the power or non-power of Alzheimer's disease. Once upon a time Enid would have knocked that woman down. If she couldn't do the job herself, she would have brought her brother, Willy the Tank.

When Enid knew a minimum amount of words, I showed her pictures in the family album, and I had quizzed her to compare her present memory with yesterday's.

"Who's this?"

"The fat one."

"That's not a nice way to describe Judy who is so kind to you."

She smiled.

"Who's this one?"

"I'm afraid."

"Why?"

She looked at me as if to say *she'd never make the mistake again and call Lloys ugly.*

"This one?"

"Cheapskate." That's how she called Taariq.

"He bought those knives to kill you?"

She smiled.

"This one?"

"He owes me money."

"Why don't you ask Nigel for your money?"

She showed no interpretive emotions.

"This one?"

"She touched the back of her dress."

"Trish mooned you to get your attention."

I turned the page. "This one?"

I didn't understand what she said.

"You *must* know this one."

She made a sign. I interpreted it.

According to my unscientific evaluation, her memory always seemed improved after we came from Nostrand Park. Or was my analysis that of a doting husband? We stood before our wedding picture on the wall, and I pointed at the bridegroom. On our wedding day I wore the style of 1959: trousers with knees space wide enough to hold Al Capone and his machine gun. In that portrait, my eyes looked into the world with hope and optimism.

"Who's this one, Fats?"

"That clown!"

My laughter echoed in the night. Mary James turned on her bedroom lights. Her southern window is a yard away from my northern window. She called out. "Is anything wrong with Miss. Crooks?" Many times Mary had gone with me to look for my wife when she walked away during her "sun downing" hour.

"No, Miss James. We are having fun."

The day ended with words of wisdom: By my *putting one foot in front and one foot behind*, as Nancy Reagan had told Larry King, and abiding by what the future may bring for the clown and his comedic wife with a brain disease that turns her derision into humor.

22

The doorbell rang with the rhythm of a tender touch. It was a young woman's touch. She was 21 years old, saddled with a backpack as heavy as Home Depot's toolkit. She wore faded jeans, a colorless pair of sneakers, and metal plugged her eardrums, probably punctured by rock and reggae music. She was the applicant for the part-time caregiver's job, advertised orally among friends.

Being her parents' friend, I interviewed her, but I had hoped the other interviewee would have come before her, and I would have had a good reason to tell this young lady "the job was already taken." She was a junior at York College. My preconceived conclusion was she would definitely not be able to handle my wife's whims, tantrums, and insults.

She rested her backpack on the floor.

"Hello, Mr. Crooks. Hello, Fats."

"Hello, Joanna. Take a seat. I'm on the

phone with my daughter, Lloys."

"Daddy, who's calling my mother *Fats*?" Lloys overheard the conversation.

I whispered into the phone, "The applicant for the job."

"Daddy, are you going to employ a woman who is calling my mother *Fats*? That's disrespectful! She's not my mother's friend."

"I'll call you later, Lloys." I hung up before she demanded to speak to Joanna.

Joanna kissed my cheek. She had kissed that identical spot when I first met her at age 17.

"Mr. Crooks, I don't usually dress like this to go on an interview, but I rushed to school to pick up my grade for my essay *Cultural Diversity*. I didn't have time to go home and change."

"All my children dressed that way once. Fats and I had worked overtime and bought new dresses for Judy and Lloys for their high school graduation. They refused to put on the new dresses. They put their gowns over their jeans. I was annoyed. That was the only graduation of my children that I had not attended, and I do not have a picture of their high school graduation. Our daughter, Gail, wore the same jeans all through college. Our son, Taariq, hid his new suit and went to his cousin's wedding in a dirty pair of jeans and muddy sneakers that he played soccer in. Consider yourself well dressed, Joanna."

She laughed, and looked herself over.

"I'll be thrilled to read your essay, if you don't mind, Joanna."

"Sure."

She unplugged her earphones and followed me into the living room. I offered her a seat, rushed to see where Fats was, and caught her before she hid behind the fridge, her latest hideout.

"Why are you hiding from me, Fats?" She kissed Fats.

"I'm glad you call her Fats. That's the name on her Alzheimer's ID bracelet. In case she walks away, give that name and the number on her bracelet to 911."

Fats sat between us.

"What's the thesis statement of your paper?"

"*Gods are good.*"

"Why that title?"

She gave me the look that I had gotten from Trich in grade school when I had asked, *why should I sign this permission slip for you to go on a field trip*?

"I'm kidding. It speaks of *destiny.*"

She handed me four loose typewritten pages. The first page had her grade. I turned the page quickly, and pretended that I didn't see her grade. Fats came closer to me as if to say, *Keep far from my husband.* I handed Fats the page with Joanna's grade even though I knew she could no longer read.

"Can I offer you something, Joanna?"

"I just had a bottle of water."

"Watching your figure?"

"I'm from a weighty family."

"Can I take Fats for a walk, Mr. Crooks?"

"She'd like that."

I read excerpts of Joanna's paper, and reread them, because somehow those excerpts told me what to expect of life, not that I didn't know, but the occasion seemed serendipitous:

God or gods may present situations that appear to involve only suffering but the ultimate goal sometimes is not to punish but to teach. The lessons learned are not only by the individuals directly involved, but essentially there is always a reason for the action of God whether or not it is readily apparent. We learn in the story of Oedipus' misfortune: that we must not try to alter destiny because the gods predetermine our fate and the inevitable will occur though alternate routes are taken. Situations are encountered where people may not look deep into an event, assume the outcome of that event is bad, and they don't recognize the greater good.

I will examine Abraham's binding of Isaac, Job, and Oedipus Rex, to give a deeper understanding.

In Genesis, Abraham was ordered by God to bind his son and kill him. Abraham was going to oblige, but God stopped him from doing so. From a certain point this may be perceived as a horrid thing, the total opposite of good. The physical actions are definitely disagreeable, but Abraham's loyalty to God— the willingness to sacrifice his son--shows that within he is good. His selflessness granted him a reward from God.

The trials that are placed before individuals like Abraham's are administered to let them see traits that are known to God, the Omniscient, but unknown to them. God wanted to test this man so He could give him the reward that God knew he deserved, but again Abraham's virtuous nature would not have allowed him to understand or accept God's gifts to him unless he felt as though he had earned these rewards. Being righteous *is hard and takes many sacrifices, but the reason prophets are loved by the mass is due to their altruistic nature.*

Job was a loyal servant of God. He, too, was recognized because he sustained a severely difficult test from God. God knew Job, and knew that Job would not fail Him. The Devil did not know this and was certain that God was wrong about Job. What would eventually happen to Job would be viewed as cruel and unjust. What Job experienced could easily direct one to conclude that God is cruel, but God is not irrational. There is reason for everything He does. It was for the greater good, because now the Devil was aware that people of God could endure trials and still in the end trust and worship God regardless of the degree of suffering they endured.

Though Job initially perceived his experience as punishment for sins, he maintained his faith in God. A lesson was learned from Job: He recognized God's nature and reaffirmed his belief in God's greatness, omnipotence, and omniscience. God, seeing this, rewarded Job with far greater gifts than he possessed before. This can only be seen as goodness and from the experiences of Job and Abraham we are reminded that though God may appear to be absent, He is always there, though it may not be noticeable. God has a plan for each of us.

The story of Oedipus parallels Job's somewhat...Oedipus' had to succumb to the prophecies of the oracle even though they thought they were capable of avoiding these things from happening...The prophecy in a way helped Oedipus or his parents get out of a terrible situation. Whom do we blame, the gods? We cannot alter destiny: what is meant to be will be.

In my opinion we should not point our fingers at the gods, instead, acknowledge their actions as an important lesson. Yes, it may seem unfair, truly evil that a family should have such an experience, but how many have learned from their misfortune?

I must therefore conclude that the gods are good; their methods of instructions are severe; but a valuable lesson is learned in the end.

The God of Abraham and Job is apparently good. Though He often tests his people, there is usually some fundamental reason that functions as a lesson to the individual being tested. In fact, he receives a reward incomparable to any other.

The gods of Oedipus function in a similar way as the God of Abraham and Job in that the delivery involves suffering. But their intentions are for the benefit of others, not necessarily those directly involved.

We learn that we can interfere, but we cannot change divine intent. If the gods ordained it to transpire, it will, despite our efforts to change the outcome.

The last paragraph of her essay won her the job.

Joanna came in. She held Fats's hand and put her on a chair. I took the page from Fats, collated the other three pages, and handed them to Joanna. "Please, make a copy for me."

"I already had my grade. Take it."

"Are you religious?"

"If compassion makes me religious, then I am."

"How many days could you work?"

"Two days, and whatever you pay me will help pay my college fee...And I'll be treating Fats and you as my grandparents."

Joanna's essay telegraphed divine intent: *Except the Lord build the house, they labour in vain that build it: except the Lord keep the city, the watchman waketh but in vain.*

She was entrenched in my employ.

Lloys, on stopover from South Africa to Canada to attend the 16th Annual Global Aids Conference in the summer of 2006 as a representative of her pharmaceutical company, said, "Daddy, I've been observing Joanna. She takes good care of my mother."

"And she no longer calls your mother *Fats*. She calls her *Mrs. Crooks*."

Joanna lived in for two weeks when I went to Florida to research Alzheimer's disease at Broward County Main Library. I was confident about her ability and kindness to Fats that I hardly called to check on her stewardship. On my return, I found a sealed letter among my mail:

Dear Mr. Crooks,

I would like to welcome you back home. I do hope you had a great vacation along with your research project for information for your book.

This has been an interesting experience. It was, at times, very difficult because I missed my husband very much. During the days it was just like when I worked on Thursdays and Saturdays only, but at nights it was extremely hard since Mrs. Crooks takes a lot of time to fall asleep, and her love for moving objects "increases after midnight." That was the worse part of this experience.

There were some very special days when I took the time to appreciate simple things of life: Humming a song together, dancing, and being called a "damn ass" by your lovely wife made me smile.

I have learned a few important lessons though: I have learned that being a caregiver requires a lot more self sacrifice than I thought. The effort is costly; the satisfaction of knowing that someone incapable of taking care of herself is made comfortable, fed, and kept clean, because of your efforts, is priceless.

Mr. Crooks, I have walked in your shoes for 2 weeks, and it allowed me to really understand that you are "indeed a hero." Though Mrs. Crooks may not be able to understand, she is one of the luckiest persons on this planet. I wish I could produce a clone of myself so she (my clone) could give you a break more frequently because you certainly deserve that.

I hope I have executed my job successfully while you were away. Stay strong. Don't forget that I am anxiously waiting to read your book about you and Fats, and laugh at the fights that you and Fats had before and after marriage.

Yours sincerely,
Joanna Haye

Our meeting was a miracle of serendipity. Since writing this letter, Joanna has earned her Ph.D. in molecular biology from Princeton University. She has given me permission to include her essay in this true story.

23

"Caleb and Kadian, your grandfather is a snake."

They are our grandchildren. They were four and six years old.

She had sent them to look for me on Nostrand Avenue. I met them at the dysfunctional traffic light.

Before they were born, nighttime was cinema time, and she was the lead actress. In hindsight, they were nights of display of her hot-flashes, too. She wore hipsters, with, or without bra. She modeled for me. Then she pretended that she was going to put on clothes.

"No, Fats. No! I like your costume."

I knew nightfall was approaching when I peered through our northern window and saw Patrick Rochester, a zealot for politics. I had gone into his shop regularly for political news. At that time he had owned R.P.D.Tailoring, a mom-and-pop establishment that sold "from a jackboot to a slipper, and more," as my mother said when she sent me to buy penny butter slapped in brown paper from Cheng Ming, the Chinese shopkeeper, who sold everything for the villagers. As Rochester lumbered home, his bald head bent, and his hobble noticeable, I prepared for our night's schedule: the arguments first, lovemaking second, sleep third.

"Fats, stop pushing me with your feet."

"You had your fun. I had no fun, and now you are snoring on me."

The street with three lampposts became quiet in winter.

One of the churches' backyards was dirty in daytime. But at nighttime that backyard looked like a theatrical scene when the flood lights were automatically lit. Stray cats were the actors and the smelly bins were their props. Darkness hid the cats' presence and reminded me when I first heard of the "sexiness of darkness."

"The sexiness of darkness gives me money," Faye had told me when we were young adults. "Darkness hides my true color and my kinky hair. And my value increases."

"Where?"

"In my darkroom?" That was her bedroom which was never lit. "You know what I do?"

"You're my friend, and that's what matters."

"Black men like girls with long hair, not my kinky hair. In the darkness, I let them touch my long wig. From a teenager, I knew men would do anything for sex." She didn't have to tell me that because I had already known the art of masturbation—having sex with myself.

I met Faye in London in 1984. "What race are you now—Indian with long hair or Negro with kinks?"

"The Englishman never asked."

We laughed as if we were at Gower's Well Road, in Fyzabad, drawing water with our buckets. "You're no good, girl."

"What about that half-breed who dumped you for the East Indian man?" She laughed as loud as a siren. "I remember you didn't eat for three months and lost a lot of weight from *tabanka*." *Tabanka* means a jilted lover's sorrow.

"I never saw her since I left Fyzabad."

"And Miss Root? Did you go back to her after your mother took you to the hospital to get circumcised?"

We laughed forever.

It was an old friendship that was renewed. There's nothing like an old friendship. I made a funny face, and Faye knew whom that facial expression represented. I said, "Bag o' Sugar," and she said, "I teased that woman every day on my way to and school, and she cursed me terribly."

A man read her newspaper over her shoulder as we traveled to East Ham by train. She tore a crescent in the page. She mashed my toes but I behaved as if I was in her darkroom and was ignorant of why she tore her newspaper. As the man stepped off the train, she said, "Limey, buy your own newspaper. Don't try to read mine."

The battle at **519** started when Enid mentioned my association with Faye.

"That's why people should not tell others of their past." I was mad as hell because I never reproached her.

Nighttime constantly reminded me of my wife's cunning: How she made me lose my sarong and my song.

John Lindsay was the Mayor then. He gave New York City a grant for every program. And I benefited from the grant he gave to Intermediate School 201 to teach jazz on Saturday. It was also the time when I feasted Enid at McDonald's every Friday night with the burger of her choice and reserved Saturday for every new date.

At McDonald's we chatted about silly things: How we'd look in old age always had an encore, with laughter. "You'd look ugly like this." "And you'd look uglier like this."

"Fats, Saturday nights with me and the boys are never enjoyable as this. Friday nights would always be yours. It's the best night of the week when I'm with you and discussing our children and having our loving chit-chats. It's better than Saturday night with the boys just talking about sports and Howard Cosel and his wig."

"I believe you." Her countenance was stoic.

Two Saturday nights passed. The third Saturday I was dressed to meet the boys.

"Seems you are dressed to eat steak instead of hamburger tonight?"

"Why do you say that, Fats?"

"Boys meeting boys don't dress that way. Nor smell that way."

"C'mon. Don't say that."

"You are not going to meet the boys tonight."

Her demeanor changed. She had already looked the doors and hid the keys.

My date, Sam, waited for me in her beat-up Ford at the intersection of the base and height of the triangle of East 26th. I saw her tail lights from the northern window.

On Thursday, Sam had shown me her disco dress with more holes than cloth and joked, "If the air conditioning unit sent breeze down my back I'd cover it with the sarong." I had bought that hand-made wrap on the Indian Strip on Lexington Avenue, New York City. "Saturday, we'll meet *on the base.*" That's how we called our meeting place.

"It's time for me to meet the boys. Unlock the door, Fats."

"Over my dead body."

Our wrangling went on and on. When I sheepishly looked through the window, the Ford was moving off from the base. Sam drove around the triangle with dimmed lights twice. Finally, she drove off to her disco party in East New York, Brooklyn.

A month later she married the man who danced endlessly with her in the disco dress.

Losing Sam was the genesis of my composition: *I'll Take Second Place, And Wait.*

Billy Gault, flautist, one of my music teachers at IS 201, invited me to his home and played my composition. "Lloyd, I like it. Why not make a demo?"

I hired Kassa, trumpeter/pianist, and his

trio, and Gia Williams, vocalist. I rented a studio in the Flatiron District of Manhattan. I paid the musicians' rates and bargained for a cut rate with Gia. She was my friend and had sung my first composition, *Sing Me Mama's Song*, in many night spots in New York, and she had introduced me as the composer of the song at Sweet Water.

A demo was cut: Gia Williams on side A, the music version on side B.

At nights I listened to my demo with earphones and hummed the last four bars as silently as the flicker of my eye lashes:

You took back your keys,
And though I know this is the end of us,
I'll take second place
And wait. And wait. And wait.

Every night I hid the tape a different place.

I came home late from my haunts. Nigel was on his drums in the basement. He was rapping and drumming.

"Fats, Nigel is great. I'm proud of him."

She smiled. "Aren't you going to show Nigel that you are proud of him?"

"After dinner."

"He said you never showed interest in him. He blamed you for sending him to Grady Vocational

School instead of Midwood High to prepare him for college."

"I went to a vocational school and learned bookkeeping, typing, and stenography. What's wrong with me? I'm making my living as a stenographer on Wall Street. I pay all the bills in this house. Just think of that. How could he say that I don't take an interest in him? I bought that new drum set and paid for his music lessons. He and I have our gigs in the living room, and you sing along sometimes."

"I apologize, honey. Please, go and hear the rap he composed."

"What you cooked?"

"When you come back from hearing your loving son's rap composition, your dinner would be steaming."

"And you know where I'd be letting off that steam later?"

"I know."

Nigel heard my pounding feet—all my children knew my footsteps whether soft or loud. He shouted, "Daddy, It's mammy who gave me."

"You sound great. Did you go to Grady today, Twiggle?" That's his nickname. He was in his last term at Grady and was behind in his program.

"Don't worry. I'd graduate, daddy." He stopped rapping.

"Are you afraid of me?"

"Daddy, it's mammy who gave it to me to record my rap. She said you don't need it any more because you had been listening to it for months."

"What are you talking about, Twiggle?"

Nigel pulled out my demo from his cassette player. He had already recorded over Side A and was almost at the end of Side B.

I screamed. I ran upstairs. I bombarded Enid with curses from my urban dictionary. I lost it that night. I ran out the house and slammed the door.

She ran to the porch and sang: *You took back your keys/ And though I know this is the end of us/ I'll take second place/ And wait/ And wait/ And wait.*

Her "*And Wait*," was sung in three octaves, and she faked her voice "into a childlike quality."

I cursed her louder.

"Same to you, Mr. And Wait."

On my way to Nostrand Park, it was as if I was in the Gulf Stream and my temperature was 18 degrees Fahrenheit hotter and angrier than anything and anybody in my surrounding. I fidgeted on the park bench. A man in the park didn't trust my mood. He left through a hole in the fence. *I am going to punish that (Redacted) for letting Nigel erase my demo.* I repeated my vengeful thoughts for the umpteenth time and stamped my feet with rage.

I never saw Sam after she took back her keys. I had imagined, every now and then, and eventually stopped imagining, that she didn't need my sarong to keep her warm; her new man did. But my anger against Enid remained. I had used my Christmas bonus from Sullivan & Cromwell to cut that demo.

I returned home after midnight, showered, and went to bed with my face to the wall.

She squeezed my hand in that special way. It was our code. Then her perfumed body was over me when she asked for my forgiveness. She was gladly forgiven.

Now when I put her in bed, and squeeze her hand, she doesn't respond to our code. So I laugh for both of us, remembering that once upon a time she outwitted me every time.

The butterfly turns back into a caterpillar.

24

There's a nameless stage in the Alzheimer's patient's life. I call that stage in my wife's life *Remember the times.*

"What's wrong with your mother?" a patient in Dr. Valasareddi's waiting room asked.

"She's my wife."

"I'm very sorry, sir."

The expressions on the other patients' faces in the doctor's office were worthy of a Norman Rockwell's.

Enid chewed constantly like a goat. That was her new habit in the late stage of AD. I put a candy in her mouth and her chewing looked normal.

The woman rose and offered Enid her seat.

"Thank you, Miss. I really need it."

"Sir, I'm so sorry for misspeaking."

"That's all right."

She wasn't the first person who thought my wife was my mother. In Key Food Supermarket on

Nostrand Avenue, Enid had walked out ahead of me. The cashier asked, curtly, "Aren't you going to pay for the bread your mother took outside?"

I looked outside and saw my wife. "Sure." The bread was under her arm the way a Frenchman holds his baquette on his way home from work. When she was lucid she would have scoffed at the sight of bread held under someone's arm.

"How are you?" I asked the woman, and squeezed myself to share the space on the chair. Getting Enid into the taxi had exhausted me. The taxi driver had helped me.

"Not happy about myself." She spoke with a welcoming smile and a lisp.

"You look fine," I said.

The patients were relieved of their discomfort by our exchange of pleasantries. They stopped turning pages of magazines that they never read.

"Looks are deceiving," she said.

She told me her name. I told her mine.

I remember the times Enid would have intervened from the outset. At a party, I had talked to a woman and had written the woman's number in shorthand in the palm of my left hand.

"Honey, here's a wet napkin." Enid looked

at the woman. "I've brought you something to eat." She opened the palm of my left hand and wiped off the woman's number.

The role is reversed now. I took out a napkin from my bag and wiped Enid's hands and mouth after she sucked the first candy. She was no longer in a state of mind to wipe my palms had I taken the woman's telephone number, but I behaved as if she were in the prime of her life. The stranger might not have given me her telephone number, but I didn't ask her to exchange numbers as I would have done in the past.

"Would you like me to take you and your wife home?"

"Wouldn't that be too much for you to do?"

"I'm driving."

Patients couldn't hide their interest in our conversation. They were the extras in our movie in Dr. Valasareddi's office.

The woman came out of the doctor's office. "My offer is still open."

"Thank you very much. But my son will be picking us up." I lied.

I remember the times when Enid would have said, "Woman, that's my (redacted) husband! What's your (redacted) problem?"

We met Gail at home. She was on the computer and multitasked with her ambient devices. She rested down her cell and went to the fridge for a soda. She came back to continue her calls but could not find her cell. She took the house phone and dialed her cell number.

Her cell rang but we could not find it. Gail hung up, and called again. Enid came from the bedroom and the cell's light flickered in her bosom like a firefly.

I remember the times when the only thing Enid put in her bosom was a hundred-dollar bill.

25

"You are back from church early, Pastor Crooks." She was in the middle stage of AD.

"Guess what I did?"

"You bought dinner for your loving husband."

"Hell no! I'll do that when you come back to church and play the piano."

"I cooked dinner for you, Fats."

"Guess what I did before I drove into the garage?" She did everything to get my attention.

"I have no idea."

"I apologized to the Russian."

"The shoemaker you said you'd *never* apologize to?"

"Yes."

"I don't believe you." I looked at her, shocked. "What made you apologize to him?"

"I am *now* a pastor. Not a backslider like you who wouldn't come to worship God."

I kept my comments to myself:*It is nine*

years since you have been the pastor of Divine Truth Assembly. I wonder if you found the church today ran through my mind.
    At bedtime she prayed for the world. She stretched her hand, and I squeezed it. She remembered our code.
    "Good night, Fats."
    "Would you play the piano for the Lord next Sunday, honey?"
    "Hell no! I'd play it for you, instead."
    She shut one eye and opened one.
    We knew what that closed eye meant. It is a toxic secret only remembered by me now.

    *   *   *   *   *   *

    Tuesday, January 31, 2006, Gloria Morancie called, and she told me about an Alzheimer's case. "John's mother died from Alzheimer's." That's not his name.
    Whenever the word "Alzheimer's" is mentioned I become a lobbyist on K Street, Washington, D.C., fronting for the drug manufacturers interested in research. I also become an imaginary roll call columnist. My column is *Tell Me What Drugs You Are Giving Your*

Patient. I am giving my Wife Aricept and Namenda.

"John wasn't giving his mother any medication," Gloria said.

"Why?" I was interested to hear John's reason.

"He said he took good care of her: He fed her, cleaned her, and had pleasant times with her. He also said he let her die a natural death because those medications would have delayed his mother's peaceful death."

"He really said that?"

"He said, had he died before her, no one would have taken care of her as he did."

Milly's advice of not giving my wife her medication crossed my mind, but I eclipsed *that* thought immediately. That thought was the Devil's.

* * * * * *

On the 50th anniversary of St. Augustine Girls' High School, the retired principal, Undine Giuseppi, writes in her memoir: "Among the special songbirds, as I called them, were Laverne Laugior, Pearl Jurawan, Kathleen Subero, and Enid Bain...." I read a clipping of the memoir to Enid as we sat on St. Jerome's Roman Catholic Church's steps, a hangout, in Flatbush, for weary feet, and Haitians who discuss Haiti's politics. It didn't matter that she didn't understand, but I read the clipping and looked into the police camera overhead. When Enid could have walked I took her there every day in summer to witness the traffic and comment on passersby especially to get her jokey replies. Now I sit there alone and think of her and look at Roman Catholic parishioners make the sign of the cross on their foreheads and chests when they pass by the church. When Enid could have talked she had said, "Why are these people worshipping a statue of Mary? Don't they know Mary is waiting on the resurrection just as everybody?" And I had replied, "Your pastor couldn't read, and you worshipped him for a long time." Then our arguments began.

In my loneliness, sometimes my mind ran on my not taking her to Bob Boross choreography class, at Hunter College. Though she couldn't speak she would have enjoyed his choreography and instructions. Bob's students danced to *What Lola Wants Lola Gets.* Anybody could have danced in his group, but I hadn't the courage to do so. Enid would have. The students' jazzy waists and shoulders went up and down as when she danced in the carnival bands in Trinidad, in micro shorts. The students' feet went forward and backward with twists as when Enid moved to proclaim the gospel of Jesus Christ, in her church. Their pirouettes were perfect as when she showed her girls that her breasts were not melted. Those thoughts "made my day." But I missed her not being with me on St. Jerome's steps. I have never missed anybody like that.

Whenever I think of her Lenten-season behavior, I'm happy.

On Ash Wednesday, February 25, 2009, Gail called from her job. "Daddy, I wish my mommy could have heard this: I told Natasha that I'm giving up something for *lent*. Natasha said she's not giving up anything to *that bitch*. I thought she was kidding. But up to when Natasha and I ended our conversation, she thought *lent* was a *man of disrepute*. I was too ashamed to correct her. My mommy would have rolled on the floor and screamed with laughter had Natasha told her that *she was not giving up anything for that bitch*."

I did not know it was Ash Wednesday. In the past I would have known because Enid would have cooked fresh fish or salted fish nonstop at the close of Shove Tuesday until Good Friday.

"Fish again, Fats?" would have been my

mantra with disgust.

"If you don't like it, lie down beside it," she would have answered.

Late Ash Wednesday, 2009, we hugged in the loveseat and listened to Tony Bennett and Barbra Streisand, in duet, on cable TV. They sang *Smile*.

That was another memory that came to me when I thought of Fats in my loneliness.

26

I experienced a *short* memory lapse twice: in our basement, and on my job. Both experiences were eerie: my senses did not function as they should. My body had given me no notice that it would have shut down.

The steel door closed on me in the basement, and suddenly I lost my memory in the stark darkness. I couldn't remember where the light switches were—switches that I had turned on and off for thirty years. My hands swam in the darkness. Drenched in fear and cold sweat, I didn't know how to think. The boiler's furnace blasted to heat the building; I saw a light switch, and turned it on. When I came out of the basement, I was still in stupor.

My second experience was on the twenty-ninth floor of the American Express Building on 125 Broad Street, New York. The floor is circular in design. I was employed by the law firm of Sullivan & Cromwell for eleven years. I went into the bathroom, did the needful, and was ready to return to my desk. Suddenly, I went blank. I couldn't visualize how I got there, and how to get back to my desk.

Am I getting Alzheimer's? I did not panic outwardly, but inwardly.

I remained on the toilet bowl. I couldn't tell how long I was there, but my fragmented senses told me if someone came in, and I had asked him how to get to my desk, that someone could have been a partner of the firm. That thought further collapsed my fractured mind.

Something was wrong with me. But how could it be?

I'd just corrected Linda Quinn's markups of a prospectus on the computer. I had intelligently answered her clients' questions. And, unlike my 17-year-old- son Taariq, a messenger at Sullivan & Cromwell, who had walked off the job because his boss had asked him to make coffee, to which he replied, "I don't make coffee in my house, and I won't %%$$## make it here for you," I, voluntarily, made coffee for Ms. Quinn. She did the same for me.

Try my innate ability for help. I remember that thought.

But I didn't know how.

Why not try your faith?

I prayed. For how long, I couldn't tell.

Somehow my memory lapse diminished slightly, and I remembered that I shared a cubicle with Elender Jones.

An idea surfaced: *The floor is circular, and from any point I would get to Elender.*

I left the bathroom and turned right. Still dumbfounded, I kept walking.

When I completed the circumference of the floor, Elender shouted, "Lloyd, where have you been? Ms. Quinn was crazy looking for her work."

Had I turned left when I exited the men's room, I would have been four footsteps away from my computer. Only a wall separated our cubicle from the men's room.

"Life is a gift from an Indian-giver," writes Francine L. Trevens, the New York poet and novelist, published by Bibliophilos. I had read her poems in 1997. I remember the year because Enid and I had a reunion with our 12-year old, grandson, Khafra, in Mozambique.

Three of us had returned from Soweto, South Africa, by helicopter. We taxied home. The cabby stopped and pointed to a little drain that Khafra could have jumped over with his eyes closed.

"What do you think that is?" the cabby asked.

"A dirty drain," Enid said.

He looked at me.

"A hole in the road, I suppose."

"Young man?"

"I don't know," Khafra answered.

The cabby said in brawling English, "In Winston Churchill's memoir, that's the river he boasted he swam across."

"That dirty, narrow drain?" Enid asked.

"That's the river that he boasted he swam across!"

He and Enid laughed until we reached our hotel. He tooted his horn, waved to us, drove off, and continued his laughter like a clown.

Enid held my hand and laughed endlessly in the lobby. I was afraid she might have thrown herself down on the floor and rolled with laughter as she did at **519**.

"Why is she laughing like that?" the concierge asked.

"Churchill's river." I, too, thought of the hydraulics of water in that dirty drain.

Other Afrikaners joined in laughter as if they were with us from the beginning of our sightseeing tour. They mocked Churchill. No doubt, they were still brooding over their loss to the British in the Boer War.

What a difference time and Alzheimer's make.

Enid is incontinent. She no longer grumbles at the woman in the mirror and shows her fist in defiance. But when she touches me I feel her love.

Alzheimer's disease has robbed her family of her joyous laughter. AD melted her pomp but molded our love. She taught me a saying she had heard, "One can't live under life, but with it."

One night I didn't sleep. I was afraid to take a *5421* because I could not remember whether I'd taken it, and the fear that I may overdose on that sleeping pill, I went without it, and did not sleep that night. Sleep, when you need it, is better than diamonds lightly got.

27

On September 23, 2006, Khafra again walked into our life. He graduated from The University of Nottingham, voted "Britain's University of the Year 2006/07." He earned a Bachelor of Science degree with honors in Cognitive Neuroscience and Psychology. As he put down his luggage he meant to practice pop psychology on me. He hugged and kissed his granny over and over, and I pressed his arms to get his attention.

"They developed from rugby in Uplands College in South Africa and from soccer in England."

In our last in-depth conversation he was 10 years old. He had told me then how he and 8-year-old Betinho, President Chissano's nephew, had gone to play soccer. When they returned to the President's gate the new guard on duty would not let them in.

"Call, Papa...Call the President" was their

contrapuntal cry.

"Whose papa?" The guard mocked them.

"He's the President."

The guard chased them away.

"You think we are nobodies?" Betinho shouted.

"Say nothing to him, Betinho. I know of a way," Khafra said softly in Portuguese.

"Was it your Brooklyn smarts that got you in?" I had asked.

"You don't want to know, Grandpa." That was his way of telling me that he would not divulge that secret.

President Chissano had told me of the incident and had said, "The guard should have called me to verify if I knew Betinho and Khafra, irrespective of their dirty appearance."

Khafra was at the front door, 21 years old. He grinned from ear to ear. "Grandpa, I've come to stay with you and granny for a year. I applied for a job to teach English in Japan. But I want you to teach me to play the piano before I leave for Japan."

I laughed.

"I'm serious, grandpa."

He knew that all my children and grandchildren

walked away from "my piano lessons." Once upon a time it was, "Can you play a Michael Jackson song, daddy? Can you play Prince? Can you play Justin Timberlake?"

"No! No! No!"

Seeing Khafra I had a happy mood. "I'd be happy to teach you, Khafra. And you can walk out on me without notice, whenever."

"I would not."

Khafra's help was invaluable. Before he came, I slept many nights in the living room, I on the couch, and Enid on the loveseat, in a sitting position. I was too tired to lift her out of the loveseat into her wheelchair and then lift her into her mechanical bed. Khafra not only became a secondary caregiver and eased my burden, but he devoured his music lessons, and switched to jazz. I always wished one of my children or grandchildren would become a jazz pianist. His Portuguese tongue gave him a craving for Bossa Nova.

He alternated on the upright piano and the keyboard and lured me into discussions the way psychologists do, I guess. The piano stool was the clinician's chair. The keyboard stool became his client's couch.

I went into my archive which is a springbok bag bought in South Africa, a gift from his mother, and pulled out all my sheet music. But I couldn't find *The Nearness of You*.

"Why that tune means so much to you, grandpa?"

"That song brought granny and me together."

"That's the only song that means a lot to granny and you?"

"No. When Johnny Nash, the American pop singer, came to Trinidad and Tobago, we went to hear him at Globe Theatre. His last rendition was *For All We Know*. That became our second favorite. I have a recording of granny singing it." I put on the tape.

"That's you accompanying her?"

"Yes."

"She never lost her beautiful voice."

"I taught her to play the piano, and she played and sang when her sister, Sylvie, died. When she came to New York she stopped playing. She was too much into church activities. *For All We Know* was the last song she sang. She sat on this very stool, on Valentine's Day, 2003, and sang it. Some months later she couldn't read, and I couldn't even get her to hum a tune.

Khafra used his artful preamble and changed the subject. "Studies have found that Alzheimer's patients who have difficulty with their memory continue to respond to music."

"Your granny held on to music for a long time because she thought it was money."

"It was *her* money."

"Is that a subtext?"

"You started it, grandpa, not me."

"Tell me something that I don't know." We laughed.

He went on the computer as if to confirm a fact: "Petr Janata, a cognitive neuroscientist and researcher at the University of California at Davis, mapped the brain activity of a group of individuals while they listened to music, and he noted activity in the medial prefrontal cortex—the area just behind the forehead (He touched the spot on my head) which covers general intelligence, sentience, and personality. That area (He touched the spot again to wake me up) is 'among the last regions of the brain to atrophy.' So in Granny's case, too, as difficulty in her memory grew, that area that I've touched continued to retain her musical ability. But as her musical responsiveness declined, her brain also declined."

He saw my confusion in understanding him fully so he switched the subject. "Aren't these chords pretty in *The Girl from Ipanema*?"

"Very pretty."

"Grandpa, do you ever think of what the future may bring?" He got off the piano.

"Yes. But I daydream mostly about how cunning your granny was."

He propped granny with pillows in her wheelchair. She no longer paced the floor with empty grocery bags held tightly in both fists. She had grown weaker with swollen feet and was medicated on *Furosemide 20 mg,* a generic drug for *Lasix*.

"Grandpa, you don't have to worry about what the future may bring. You have given granny love, and love multiplies love. You are here for her, and I will be here for you. The future brought me. I am not putting myself in front of your children, but I'm here, too."

I was touched by his sincerity, but I didn't look up at him. My eyes looked at the floor; and I shook my head and thought of him as the kid I gave piggyback home after gallivanting with him in strange homes and places.

28

At 2:15 p.m., Saturday, January 13, 2007, Joanna took Enid to the bathroom. I was editing Enid's story on the computer. Joanna screamed, and I rushed to the bathroom and saw that she struggled to keep Enid under control. Enid's upper extremities shook uncontrollably. We held her firmly and lowered her to the floor.

She had her first seizure.

Joanna called 911 for an ambulance.

"Keep the patient lying on her side," the person who received the call said.

As I rode in the back of the ambulance to Downstate Medical University Hospital of Brooklyn, I knew my wife's tomorrows would never be healthy as her yesterdays. An oxygen mask covered her nose, and her eyes were glued on me.

She remained in the hospital for five days and was unable to walk.

* * * * *

Dr. Howard A. Crystal, Professor of Neurology and Pathology, Director, Division of Behavioral Neurology, SUNY Downstate Medical Center, her outpatient doctor, writes:
[Certain information omitted.]
"February 2007
"RE: CROOKS, Enid
"HISTORIANS: History was provided by her husband.
Mrs. Crooks is a 73-year old right-handed woman who was seen briefly in the clinic at Suite C and I indicated I would care for her here.
"HISTORY OF PRESENT ILLNESS: Her husband indicated that she has had a 20-year history of progressive dementia. He said it was diagnosed 10 years ago. She has been unable to speak at all for about one or two years. She has been incontinent for two years or three years. She has required help to walk for at least a year. Food has to be placed in her mouth, but she will swallow it on her own. She sleeps 10 hours at night in a separate bed from her husband in the same room.

She awakens at 10 a.m. He washes her, dresses her, and brings her down to breakfast. She spends much of the rest of the day in her chair.

    She had an episode of falling to the ground with generalized shaking and trembling of both upper extremities without loss of consciousness in January 2007. She was admitted to UBH neurology service [and] was about to be discharged when she had another episode, at that time with "foaming and frothing" at the mouth. She was cared for by Dr. Greenblatt and by Dr. Soma.

    A CT scan of her head showed atrophy. I do not have the results of an EEG. She was started on *Dilantin* and then switched to *Neurontin* 250 mg/5 ML; 300 mg (i.e. 6mL) three times a day. On that regimen, she had no further episodes. She also takes *Namenda* 10 mg twice a day. She had been on a cholinesterase inhibitor, but is no longer. Her husband has home health aides two days a week, which he pays for.

"SOCIAL HISTORY: She was born in Trinidad and came to the United States when she was 35 years old…and was a pastor.

"FAMILY HX: Her father died at 80 with dementia.

"PHYSICAL EXAMINATION: General appearance: Her eyes are closed much of the time. She would open her eyes and occasionally seemed to follow for a few seconds. Later, however, with her eyes open, she did not react to a dollar bill. She did not respond to her name. She withdrew bilaterally to pain. She was mute.

"CRANIAL NERVE EXAM: Face was symmetric. She had full range of lateral eye movements.

"MOTOR EXAM: Showed 3+ tone with bilateral upper extremity drifts. She has no tremors. There is no cogwheeling. There were no grasp reflexes.

"DEEP TENDON REFLEXES: 2+

"PLANTARS: The toes were bilaterally downgoing.

"IMPRESSIONS: Mrs. Crooks appears to have end-stage dementia, most likely due to Alzheimer's disease. At first, her husband indicated that some inappropriateness such as withdrawing money from the bank was an initial symptom raising the possibility of frontotemporal dementia. However, on further questioning it seems less likely.

This could be an early-onset Alzheimer's disease with a presenilin mutation or she could be homozygous for E4.

I suggested to her husband that we have a discussion about disease modifying therapies and risk of dementia with her children. Perhaps we will have it at the next visit."

I told my children what Dr. Crystal said. Taariq gave me the reason why he didn't care to see Dr. Crystal. "Sir, insurance companies and employers have a way of finding out your medical history. I don't intend to stay on my job forever as much as I like it. If there's a mere suspicion of dementia in me, and I apply for another job, my condition would not be sacred in this digital age."

In high school, Taariq had read *Dossier--The Secret Files They Keep on You* written by Aryeh Neier. That book speaks about the secret files government keeps on its citizens. Undoubtedly, that book changed his "trust in privacy concerns in the hands of others." Judy said she's considering going to Dr. Crystal. My other children have not given me a reason why they have not seen him, or any other doctor about "disease modifying therapies and risk of dementia" in their future.

In April 2010, Enid had another seizure and was put on *Levetiracetam 550 mg* tablet, generic for *Keppra;* that dosage was reduced to *250 Levetiracetam mg.*

29

Khafra lifted granny to put her in bed, then he put her down to sit. "Grandpa, it is ten-thirty. You always played *My Funny Valentine* for granny on Valentine's Day. You didn't play it today."

I sat at the upright piano. I played one bar, then two. Then tears blocked my vision. I cried aloud.

Khafra rushed and put granny in bed. He didn't trust my mood. He sleeps upstairs and studies Japanese in his room. That night he put his chair next to mine, and he encouraged me to watch a movie with him. But I noticed he didn't care about the movie. "Grandpa, how long would you be able to handle granny?"

"As long as ever. But I would never put her in a nursing home."

He began his pop psychology to make me laugh. "Grandpa, when I was a little boy, long before I went away to live in Mozambique, I had asked you, 'Why you had a child with another woman?' You replied then, 'When you get older I'll tell you.' I'm 21, aren't you going to tell me? Even if granny hears, she cannot curse you as she used to."

He laughed. I laughed. We were a laughing duet.

Still laughing, I said, "I'll tell you the truth if you'll allow me to tell people what you said about Jesus when you testified in granny's church when you were seven years old."

"Don't ever repeat that to anyone. If I find that tape, I'll burn it."

At age seven, I took him everywhere, and he remembered a lot about me, and my women friends, but I always behaved properly in his presence.

"Tell me why I love granny more now compared to when we were young?"

It was as if Khafra wanted me to ask that question.

"When Granny was Granny, she was your boss, just as her mother was her father's boss, and her grandmother, Teacher Evie, was her husband's boss. Granny inherited her mother and grandmother's bossiness. Sorry to say, grandpa, but you and the other two men were under your wives' jurisdiction somewhat afraid." He paused. "Granny, having lived with those two women, their behaviors and roles became etched in Granny's character and personality. This ingrained behavior did not allow Granny to be put in a position of weakness and let someone take care of her.

"You told me the story of Teacher Evie, the Spiritual Baptist Pastor, who butted a member of her church into submission because he wouldn't shut up when she preached.

"My Granny is a chip off that block and always felt inclined to assume the role of the leader, caretaker, and rock of the family, as her mother and grandmother did. Her immutable behavior limited the roles that you, grandpa, could play, not only to your family, but for Granny as well. In limiting your expression, Granny limited your appreciation to express your emotions. But now that Granny is no longer able to pursue that behavior, owing to the progression of the Alzheimer's, and she is now forced, unconsciously, to accept weakness, you are able to express yourself and assume different roles in her life.

"This freedom allows you to categorically appreciate how you feel about Granny. I look at the way you adore Granny. This freedom leads you to believe that your love is stronger than before, whilst it may be a case of your love finally finding the modes of expression that it *so* desired.

"You said Granny yearned to own a church to compete with her siblings. I always disagreed with that statement but I was too young to intervene at that time. I don't think that Granny built her biblical knowledge, her church, and her congregation to compete with her siblings' successes in education and wealth. Everyone enjoys recognition, and Granny is no exception. In your countless recordings of her sermons I hear and feel her enthusiasm and genuine love of reaching out to people and showing them a road to transformation through God.

"Granny's love for reaching out to people didn't subside when it conflicted with her economic security. That is the ultimate test of a person's love of their craft—hers was the teaching of the Gospel of Jesus Christ.

"She paid for her church out of her own pocket, and prayed for customers in debt at her workplace and risked losing her job. And you know her job was her bread and butter, and even I was the benefactor of her bread and butter. If this was all a ruse, she would have separated her financial security from the onset. Dedicating that much time, energy, and money, while raising six children, and inviting the possibility of financial problems, just to be *one up* on her siblings, would be a Pyrrhic victory.

"I remember when I came from Mozambique on holiday, and you had enrolled me in Sheepshead Bay High School to kill time, you had told me the meaning of Pyrrhic victory. I remember everything you taught me.

"Granny may have enjoyed the feeling of besting her brothers and sisters, but not at the expense of other people—that of her sons and daughters." He brushed dust off my shoulder. There was nothing to brush.

"Khafra, this is my first time on a psychologist's chair."

"I'm not a chartered psychologist, grandpa"

"How do you consider yourself?"

"Just your grandson."

"Soon, grandson, I'll be having my second prostate proceduro."

"When?"

"Dr. Rudberg would let me know…And when do you assume your teaching assignment in Japan?"

"I'm waiting on a letter. But I will be going to Taiwan first."

"Girlfriend?"

He smiled. "We met at Nottingham's."

"That's all."

His smile broadened. But I knew I'd have to pull his teeth to get more than a smile.

The next morning he lifted granny off the bed and cradled her to walk, step by step, while I prepared breakfast. This was our routine.

He let her go to see if she could stand upright by herself. The process went on for a month.

I shouted for joy one morning. "Fats, you can walk!" She made one step, then two.

The dirty ceiling looked ritzy that morning. Hope was on the way. But she only walked for a short time.

30

When I began this chapter, Enid was covered by Medicare (National Government Services, Inc.) and by United Health Care Service LLC, as a retiree of Consolidated Edison Inc. I never understood which insurance covers what. On the day Enid was discharged from Downstate Medical Hospital, the social worker told me Enid's benefits as an outpatient:

1. Six visits from a nurse.
2. For the first week, the home healthcare attendant would come 3 hours for 3 days.
3. For the second week, the home healthcare attendant would come 3 hours for 2 days.
4. For the third week, the home healthcare attendant would come 3 hours for 1 day.
5. A mechanical bed (on loan).
6. A wheelchair (on loan)

"Mr. Crooks, here's a list of nursing homes. If your wife is transferred from here to a facility of your choice, the mechanics of a transfer would be easier than from your home."

"I think I'll do it from here." I really meant to say *probably I'll do that after discussion with my children when I get home.* But my discussion with the social worker ended with a blast of "No! No!"

"No! No! Daddy, you are heartless to my mother!" Judy shouted. She cried aloud and called her brothers and sisters on her cell.

Lloys called from South Africa first. "Daddy, I've been unkind to you in the past, but I'm asking you now for your *forgiveness.* I know it has been tough taking care of my mother for all these years. But, please, bear with my mother for another six months. If her condition worsens--and I heard she cannot walk since the seizure--then...." Her voice trailed off. She was crying.

Trish called from North Carolina. Although she did not tell me, I knew Gail, her partisan, was clandestinely hooked on conference call. I wouldn't be surprised if her brother, "Professor Nigel," as he was called by Mary James, also listened on a conference hookup. They are the Three Buddies. If one says *hold* the other two say *cut.* Those were my mother's words before a flogging when Paul and I played hooky from school and ate our lunch by TLL pond.

"Daddy, are you really going to do that?" Trish refrained from saying *Put my mother in a nursing home.*
"I'll call you back, Trish."
"Daddy, I want an answer *now.*"
"The way your mother looked on the floor when she had the seizure...I don't know if I could handle her in that condition at home. Please, give me some time to think."
Trish would not let me hang up.
At eight years old, I had punished her for impertinence to Mrs. Victor, her teacher, and she wrote me a letter and told me why I was wrong to punish her. That letter is glued to the wall as her many other letters of defiance. I put her to stand in the hallway on another occasion when she was rude Mrs. Victor. She shouted: "You are not an American! Go back to Trinidad where you came from... I told you to cut off the ends of my bread, and you forgot to do that for my breakfast. I told you to take out the white from my eggs, and you forgot to do that, too. That is why I threw my shoes below the bus today again." She hated Clark shoes because they lasted too long. My mind drifted to the past as Trish hammered me on not putting her mother in a nursing home. But I also remembered

her anger when eight years old when her mother disagreed with her. "Mammy, I'm waiting for you to get old to slap you." Enid's eyes welled, and Trish said, without hesitation, "Mammy, don't cry. You know you and your Bookey always make jokes with one another." Her mother called her Bookey.

Trish "never subscribed to dutiful obedience." So I knew with her "accessible language" that she wouldn't hang up the phone, at my request, at a time when she thought that I was negotiating to put her mother into a nursing home.

In a flashback I saw her as the 3-day old baby, brought from Brooklyn Hospital, in blankets, cuddled by her mother. Then I saw her again, with her siblings on the bed with their mother when she demanded her mother's attention. Judy had said then, "Don't forget you were adopted, little girl. Keep that in mind when you try to get my mother's attention." She replied, "Don't forget that you are fat, and your fat took your senses, fat girl."

Their mother was the captain who controlled our children's disagreements. The bed-head was the bridge of the ship where their mother steered our children's likes and dislikes, their religious beliefs, their reasoning.

She sensed that my mind had strayed, and

she shouted, "Daddy, are you listening to me? What are you going to do with *my* mother?"

"I'll call you back within the next five minutes. I have to ask the social worker a few more questions...." I dare not end the sentence with *about a nursing home.* I felt her mood over the phone. Years gone, once a month her mother and I sat in judgment around the dining table and let our children say what they don't like about us. Trish was the *only* child who censured our behavior and demanded that we increased her allowance.

Taariq stood next to me in the hallway as doctors and nurses passed by. "Sir, whatever you decide, I'm on your side."

I walked away and counseled myself.

Then I made my first phone call: "Lloys, I am *not* going to put your mother into a nursing home." I felt her sigh of joy.

In thirty-second intervals, every child called me and thanked me.

"Sir, whatever was your decision that would have been all right with me," Taariq said, repeatedly.

No one said, *Daddy, from now on, I'll be there to help you with my mother some nights because taking care of her all through the night is a tough job.*

Nonetheless, even though I had no intention of putting my wife into a nursing home, I wanted to know the procedure of putting her into a nursing home and the cost of her upkeep. One never knows what the future may bring. I had told my children "not to feel guilty should the need arise to put me into a nursing home because I enjoy hospital food."

In group therapy there were "side bars" by caregivers when counselors discussed "Paying for healthcare...Medicaid insurance coverage is better to have in some instances...Medicare rarely pays for respite for Alzheimer's patients."

Caregivers in group therapy voiced their fears: "An Alzheimer's patient got to be dirt poor for the Administration to put him on Medicaid...I know of a man who divorced his Alzheimer's wife so that she'd be put on Medicaid in order that their house wouldn't be taken away to pay for her healthcare costs...What's the use of sacrificing all your life and then the little you have left would be taken away when you fall sick in old age?...Don't the politicians know of the medical crisscrosses in old age?...You know of a good Elder Law attorney? I need their advice...Medicare is a government's benefit but it only goes so far where a nursing home is concerned."

I visited a nursing home to prove the point that "Medicaid would have been a better insurance than Medicare had I put my wife into a facility." And to further prove that one has to be "dirt poor to be put on Medicaid."

An official welcomed me warmly and gave me a tour of her company's facility. The surroundings were clean. The patients were tidily dressed. Some played dominos and card games. One patient slept in her wheelchair, her head popped up and down. I wondered how long she was in that awkward position and whether she had eaten and had her pampers changed.

The official said, "Mr. Crooks, if you are satisfied with our nursing home, call the Administrator in Admittance tomorrow. Tell her the truth when she interviews you because she has to verify *the Look Back Period*."

"To see if I'm a criminal?" She was in no mood for senseless banter. Her eyes could tell.

"To see if your assets--yours and your wife's--qualify your wife to change from Medicare to Medicaid to pay your expenses at this home. Medicaid *may* give you the full benefits of the facility without subjecting you to *other things.*"

What other things? I now see why Elder Law attorneys are needed came to mind.

The Admittance specialist came directly to the question of finance when I called the following day. She added the totals of our pensions, social security benefits, monies in the bank, and rental income.

I heard her calculator. It stopped. She spoke. "This total as of today would be used in my calculations. If you deplete your savings in the banks after this call, the amount of monies in your banks as of today would be used in my calculations. Other checks would be made."

"If we use the money we have to pay off the mortgage on the house we are living in...."

I heard her calculator again. "Everything *so far* is based on what is reported today."

She said something else based on the regulations but I did not understand what she said.

"If we apply the regulations this way—based on what I explained before--you would be eligible for a monthly allowance...." She called the figure.

"For what?"

"To live on."

"Why that little money? I have other bills to pay."

She explained how she arrived by that "money figure." I, too, probably had Alzheimer's-at-that-moment because I forgot what she told me.

Her legalese turned me into a paraglider pulled to higher heights by the suction of her voice which was like a thunder storm of confusion. I still didn't understand her different explanations.

"Who owns the house you live in?" she continued.

"I own one-third."

"When was your wife's name taken off the deed?"

"Three years ago."

"That changes the application of the regulations: Now I'll have to base my *new* calculations as if your wife *still* owns one-half of the property. Any property she sold or owned less than five years ago will be tied in our calculations before any consideration for Medicaid could be considered."

She sensed that I was not on the same page with her and explained again the requirements needed by my wife to change from Medicare to Medicaid. She spoke as slowly as she could. I only understood that my wife's social security and pension would *not* be sufficient to pay for her upkeep in the nursing home, and that "other payments" would have to be found.

In group therapy I learned what "other payments" meant.

I had my pantomime moment. My audience was my voice and my conscience: *Our sacrifice to own our property and live as decent people would be naught. We are old. We are not rich. We paid our taxes. We survive on checking plus from Chase and have to pay Chase's interest. Why must we give away our house?*

I was lost in my thoughts but I heard a voice.

"Mr. Crooks, do you understand? I have to go back into *the Look Back Period* of five years to verify your and your wife's receipts and expenditures before I can give you an answer of whether she can be granted Medicaid Insurance."

I mumbled: "Do politicians who ask for our votes know people's medical crisscrosses in old age?" I plagiarized what I had heard in group therapy.

"Could you speak louder? I heard you already had a tour of our nursing home by our secretary. Let me know when you'd be coming in to discuss the matter with me, finally."

"I'd let you know. Thank you very much."

A wall plaque given me by Nicole Thébaud drew my attention: **Be kind to your children...for they will choose your nursing home.**

I didn't go back to the nursing home to be interviewed by the Administrator because I will never put Fats into a nursing home. So I still do not know if it is true that people, my age, with little means, would have to surrender their house earned through blood, sweat, and tears, before they are put on Medicaid.

31

The bedside clock read 10 a.m. on Sunday, February 18, 2007. Iraq dominated the airwaves, and the spin doctors repeated how wrong they could be about everything.

I dreaded the task before me. I had spent the night plugging away at *Ice and Eyes in the Sun* until 4 a.m. I lay in bed and hoped at least one of our children would come and relieve me for the day.

A caregiver's story advised: "The primary caregiver should not wait on family members to volunteer their help. The primary caregiver should *designate* who should do what. Don't make mother's caregiving a volunteer enterprise."

If nobody came to my aid, I'm to be blamed. I behaved as if I'm Superman. "Do not come. I can manage. Whenever I need you, I'll let you know."

This behavior was wrought from childhood

by way of my mother. In the direst of circumstances, she never asked for help. And if someone helped her on his own volition, she'd be forever grateful. She always prayed for Mr. Cheeseman who bought the *First Primer* for Paul, and all her children learned to read from that book.

Khafra saw how slowly I moved. "I'm here to help, grandpa." He lifted granny, put her on her feet, and held her firmly.

I made breakfast, and rushed around as a "Portuguese midwife," a term my mother used when she rushed around and made breakfast for my stepfather.

Khafra held granny's hands and moved her gently to get her to step off. He stopped at the breakfast table, stood behind her, and left her to stand by herself. She swayed. I rushed forward.

"What the hell is wrong with you, boy?" He hated when I called him boy, but all he said was "Shoo."

Granny swayed and stopped. We looked at her: My heart was in my mouth; his confidence was in his voice: "Move, granny."

I moved closer to her. He signaled not to interfere.

What if she falls...What would I tell the doctors at Downstate Emergency?

Breakfast was like my mother's when life was kind to her when my stepfather moved in: bits of cooked, left-over chicken, beef, and anything meaty, dumped in the iron pot, with chopped onion, big-leafed thyme, sprinkled with a tip of salt, a touch of hot pepper sauce, and other this-and-that seasoning. I let my recipe consommé for three minutes. The aroma must have pierced granny's nostrils which looked larger with her weight loss.

She made two steps to the breakfast table... two more. She tilted forward, and I held her in an embrace.

Like Polyhymnia, the muse of psalmody and religious song, I shouted, "Thank God!"

Khafra looked at me as if God were foreign in my vocabulary.

"Do you think she'll make four steps tomorrow, too?" I asked.

"Life is trial and error, grandpa."

"Your granny proved that."

He whipped out a sheet of paper from his pocket. "This is the congratulatory letter from the Nova Group, dated March 6, 2007, to teach English in Japan. I have to be there in June."

"Good luck. I'll miss you so much." I hid my sorrow because I knew none of our six children could fill the gap he left.

32

Fats and I were denied entrance to our love nest because Alston changed the lock to his apartment for the second time. We had abused his bedroom again. We walked beneath the moonlight and shuffled by pumping jacks and oil rigs until we met the darkest spot on the private road in NMC (National Mining Company). We sat on "our log" indented by our bodies. That became our hotel. Fyzabad had no hotels. Even if there were, I would not have been a patron because nothing in Fyzabad was kept a secret, and I had my bedroom eyes on another city girl who came to live near my parents.

On the log I did every thing that would make Fats giggle. But she did not. She was in a strange mood. I was talking about sex, and she was talking about the problems that come after sex.

"Are you pregnant, Fats?"

"No."

"Then why talk like that?"

"Mom said when she lost her twins the pain was excruciating. If I have that kind of pain after my first child that would be my last."

"Pain builds character, Fats."

"Probably for you, not for me. I'm even afraid of menstrual pain."

"Your mother had six children so the pain was probably nice."

"What?"

"If childbearing were that painful you would not have been born."

"Take me back to Miss Vio. I don't want to listen to more of your nonsense." Violet was her landlady.

"How many children would you have for me?"

"I wouldn't do like Mom and have six if the first gives me unbearable pain."

"Pain builds character, girl."

"You learned that foolishness from atheist John Jules? You ever had real pain?"

"When a boy in Trinidad and Tobago and the dentist pulled my teeth at the health office."

"You are comparing that to Mom's childbearing pain? She was groaning in our house for hours, and you could have heard her miles away."

I didn't answer.

"When your time comes to handle pain, just don't hide it from me if we are living in the same house."

The time she forecast came on Tuesday, July 24, 2007. But she couldn't talk to remind me of what I said on the road to NMC.

On Monday, July 23, 2007, I had my second urological procedure for an enlarged prostate, BPH (Benign Prostatic Hypertrophy), in Dr. Rudberg's clinic.

Patricia DeCoteau, RN, who acts as my *Merck Manual of Medical Information*, explained what my doctor did:

"Mr. Crooks, you'd find me using the word *enable* many times. It is to make my explanation as simple as possible.

"Your procedure was a TURP (Transurethral Resection of the Prostate). It was done for dilation of the prostate. It enabled easy access for relieving obstruction. The procedure enabled your urine to pass through the urethra without any discomfort. A Foley (catheter) was inserted into your penis during the procedure to enable you to pass urine freely for at least 72 hours, and the Foley would be removed when your doctor feels you are able to void (pass urine) without difficulty or without assistance." She paused. "You'd be having a new stream, a sensational stream." She quipped as her deceased father, Uncle Dee. "When is your doctor going to remove the Foley?"

"Thursday, July 26."

On Tuesday, July 24, the Foley was blocked with blood clots that had to be irrigated to enable easy access for my urine to flow.

It was the first time in my life that I had such excruciating pain. Words couldn't describe that pain, and I wondered if that's what Fats had called "real pain" when I spoke glibly about pain in Fyzabad lovers' lane.

Taariq and Judy rushed me to the clinic. Dr. Rudberg and his nurse tried to irrigate me but were unsuccessful because of my constant spasm.

I thought of euthanasia and wished Dr. Jack Kevorkian was my doctor instead. Yet I thought of who'd take care of Fats if I killed myself or got assistance from Dr. Kevorkian. Before I left home I had kissed her, and the agony of pain contorted my face. She looked at me as Taariq lifted me, and I barely touched her face to signal goodbye.

"Dr. Rudberg, please, call an ambulance to take me to the hospital where you work. I cannot stand this pain any longer. I'd rather die."

"Coney Island Hospital is the nearest hospital from my clinic, and that's where the ambulance would take you. I work at Long Island College Hospital, downtown Brooklyn."

"I'll take him there," Taariq said. He eased me off the bed. He put on my pants, looked at the hanging catheter, and frowned. He probably thought had he continued his physician assistant studies in college instead of switching his major to technical studies he would have been able to make the right decision and would have taken me to the nearest hospital before coming to Dr. Rudberg's clinic.

Taariq's Hyundai Sonata's tires screeched as he drove off Oceanview Avenue, Brighton Beach, in the heart of "Little Odessa." I thought of how Fats couldn't say, to my displeasure, and her ire, as when she could talk, "Ha! Ha! I had pain with six children...Pain built my character, why not yours now?"

The way I looked she would have been

sympathetic and would not have mocked me. Before AD, she remembered every unkind word I had told her. When I left the house, she was ripping the hem of her dress. My condition meant nothing to her.

The smell of Taariq's hot tires was in my nostrils. The needle of the speedometer read 91, 92, 93, 94, 95, and I kept moving from side to side with pain. He broke every red light. I waited to hear the sirens in pursuit. Disappointment is good, sometimes. No police cars were nearby.

On the Gowanus Expressway, he said, "Daddy, we'll soon be there." I wiggled more, dug my feet into the car's carpet, inhaled and exhaled. My antics increased the pain.

I saw Judy in the rearview mirror. She sat on both hands and hoped, I thought, that the weight of her body on her hands would decrease the speed of the Hyundai. She, too, was in pain—a different kind, I surmised: If the Hyundai crashed, and she died, would her sons, Caleb and Kadian, be fed on time? She feeds them before and after meals. "Calorie compensation" is their diet: If her boys had a balanced meal in the morning, they did extra food junking with "vanishing caloric density" at night. I love her equally with my other six children.

But love and pain are not synonymous.

The view was scenic but it meant nothing to me as when I toured with visitors from overseas. Manhattan skyscrapers lit the sky in the distance. I had learned a trick to combat pain from my mother, suspect as it was: When we came from the fields and the weight of the load on my head was as heavy as lead, she said: "Blackboy, count from one to a hundred, say the letters of the alphabet backwards, and memorize your five-time tables to come first in test. I did not believe her then because the heavy bundle of wood and provision on my head hurt until I unloaded them. And I never came first in test either because Sheila Henry always came first. Yet I tried to count the glowing bulbs on the Verrazano Narrows Bridge, "built for the curvature of the earth," to take my mind off suicide. *Stoppage of water is hell.*

A minute later I froze because I thought the car would crash.

The force of the wind from a 45-foot tractor-trailer in the adjacent lane pulled the Hyundai towards it like a slow magnet. Taariq went with the current of the wind and roared pass the giant 18-wheeled rig that transported food to Brooklyn. Its bold sign on its broadside said its purpose.

A sudden lift of the Hyundai put us into another lane, and by the cadence of its wheels I knew the musical sonata on the Expressway ended to the tune of bumps on the service road, and I saw Long Island College Hospital.

It was 2:00 A.M., Wednesday, July 25. Taariq lifted me out of his car. Judy supported me and guided me to the triage to register, and then I was taken to the emergency room.

Jessica, the physician assistant, heeded Dr. Rudberg's advanced call of my arrival. She had a bed for me after I was booked in the triage. I looked at her and bit into my lips. She is a pretty young woman, about 30 years, 5-feet-1, about 90 pounds. A male nurse accompanied her to my makeshift bed, separated from others by a screen.

"Mr. Crooks, I'm putting morphine in your drips," the male nurse said.

"Put as much as you want to get rid of my pain." I mustered strength to say that.

"The other medication is for the spasm, Mr. Crooks."

Gloved, Jessica began the irrigation of the Foley to clear the clots in my bladder. I watched attentively. She flushed normal saline into my bladder, clamped the Foley, released it after a couple seconds, and blood clots flowed out. She continued the irrigation process for forty five minutes or more. Then, as if she were in cahoots with Houdini, the pain was gone.

"Thank you, Jessica." My voice rose in quick crescendo.

Taariq pushed the screen and walked in without Jessica's permission. "Everything's okay, daddy?" He usually calls me *Sir*, but I felt special when he called me *Daddy* for the second time in one night. He, too, thanked Jessica. We later learned her full name was Jessica Rivati before marriage.

"I'll come back later today and see you, sir." Taariq reverted to his normal salutation.

In the wee hours of the morning, I couldn't help but go over my life as I lay in bed. Soliloquizing is a habit developed from childhood. I thought about how Fats, when she first fell in love with me, looked out of Miss Vio's window and ran down the hill and met me under Fyzabad moonlight. Those memories and what Fats and I did on the log in NMC dimpled my cheek, but the last flashback was horrible. My heart palpitated as if I were reliving that horrible day: I had slipped out of my job at Sullivan & Cromwell to withdraw money from

Chemical Bank (now Chase), 55 Water Street, New York, New York. I had exited through the northern revolving door at 125 Broad Street, onto the Vietnam Memorial Plaza. That is the plaza where the Vietnam soldiers were welcomed and greeted ten years after they returned from the war. The soldiers had walked over the Brooklyn Bridge to get to Vietnam Memorial Plaza. From the Plaza, I strolled into Chemical Bank.

I filled a withdrawal slip and endorsed my pay check. First, I pushed in my check to the teller. Then I flipped the withdrawal slip. The teller barely held the breadth of the withdrawal slip when I recognized inked writing on it that said: I HAVE A GUN. HAND ME THE MONEY.

I pressed my index, middle, and ring fingers on the withdrawal slip and prevented the teller's finger from pulling the slip in.

"Something's wrong, sir?" she asked.

"Let go my check!"

She pushed out my payroll check and the withdrawal slip and looked at me. She pursed her mouth to say *something*—It wasn't have a nice day, sir. She swallowed whatever that *something* was, and said, "Next in line."

I rushed out of the bank and tore up the

withdrawal slip and dropped the scraps a distance away from the bank and in three different roadside bins. Fright took over my body that lunch time. My belly groaned. Liquids squirted out from within. My saliva parched. "Who'd believe I didn't go to rob the bank? I would die in jail because I couldn't handle that shame to my family."

I rushed home that evening to my wife—it was not a habit of mine—to tell her what had happened in the bank. Enid went on her knees and took me down with her. She wasn't **519**'s clown that evening. She was Pastor Crooks. She called on God for me. "Thank you, God. You know my husband is not a bank robber."

I half slept in the comfort of her arms that night. But I thought of what could have been the outcome at the bank. *Who would believe my story? Who would not?*

Next payday I meant to reward my prayerful wife. I went back to said Chemical Bank on Water Street and cashed my payroll check, but I inspected the withdrawal slip thoroughly and went to a different cashier. From Water Street, I turned left on Wall Street, right on Broadway. I looked at the Merrill Lynch building and remembered Fats once worked at Merrill, and we had lunch dates there. I continued on Broadway and turned on Canal Street. I was in the heart of China Town. The brisk walk took 20 minutes.

The dress racks on Canal Street were laden. I liked my choice for my beautiful wife. It was summer. I thought of how she'd wear my choice with style. We'd go in Prospect Park by the lake. No. We'd go by the bandstand on the other side of the lake and listen to Latin bands and dance to be seen. Then we'd have juicy hamburgers, bitten in unison. We'd talk about how our children have grown and have changed their habits. I foresaw the whole day: My wife would wear the dress I bought. She'd love it. She'd boast to her friends at Con Edison, "My husband bought me a beautiful dress."

I made my choice and walked to the clerk. "This dress is for my wife. I've already bought a gift bag. I have to catch the train to Brooklyn."

"Good choice. You're a good man," the sales clerk said.

The train conductor announced: "Church... Beverley...Newkirk."

"That's my stop." I ran up the subway steps.

I was 135 pounds then and never huffed and puffed. In a jiffy I was home.

"Fats, I bought you something nice. Here."

"Let me give you a big kiss. Let me give my husband two kisses more and something later tonight." Her lipstick stamped three lips on my face.

She took the gift out. She saw it with one eye motion and said, "Take this %%$$& $8 dress from China Town for one of your ugly women. You ever see me wear these cheap dresses."

That night was *not* a lovely tune.

My flashbacks ended. The moment became current when the man on the bed next to me snored aloud. It seemed he snored louder at the approach of daylight beneath hospital sheets.

I looked at the Foley. I had no pain. I dressed and waited for Taariq.

*   *   *   *

Taariq drove into the driveway. He looked at my hospital gown. He never thought I would have been discharged the same day so he brought no clothes for me. He turned off the engine.

"Thank you, Taariq. I know you are tired

after those long shifts on your job."

He knew I was about to be emotional so he stopped me.

"Sir, what's the use of your three medical insurances when the hospital discharged you in less than 24 hours? Couldn't they keep you a day longer to see if your pain would recur?" He looked at the Foley.

"The doctors probably knew I wanted to go home to take care of my wife."

"That's what it is?" The way he smiled I knew he was happy that I was discharged.

"Did you remember my wish if I had died?"

"Cremate your body. Put on your wife's tombstone *I fell in love with that guy from Fyzabad.*"

"Remember I don't want speeches. I've already written my eulogy to be read by my grandchildren. You know where it is?"

"It is stuck on the wall with your DNR instructions"

"Do not resuscitate. So you remember."

He helped me out of his car and up the steps. I walked into the bedroom and shouted, "Fats, where are you? Did you know I slept out last night?"

She was in bed. Her eyes spoke of her joy

seeing me.

Once upon a time a war at **519** would have begun as I stepped inside. She would have clocked my jaw, and I would have run. Now she was as silent as the thoughts in the *cul-de-sac* of her mind.

Khafra was right: "My love is finally finding the modes of expression that it so desired."

I can say, without a caveat, "I love you truly, Fats. I was always your lover. But your Alzheimer's condition makes you my lover now. And I'm ashamed of waiting this long to reciprocate your boundless love for me."

The Nearness of You is my signature tune, and I make as many mistakes as when I first played it 53 years ago. The only difference is: I've come to the realization that she tricked me in the post office. She already knew the song, but she used ignorance to outsmart me to get into my life.

"Go, girl! Do it again in our hereafter."

In literature we reach places and meet people. In love, "we kill two birds with one stone"—*to love* and *to be loved* polishes the stone.

Mammy's favorite saying was, "Hollis, mud huts can fool the sun, but not the rain." Today, I'm not afraid of the rain because I have nothing to hide. And I still look at the sun for strength and to remember Paul.

Giving my wife my love on the last journey of her Gethsemane is the best social call that I've answered. Once, like bees, she never got lost. Now she is; and I will continue to be her seeing-eye dog to the end of her days, if I do not predecease her.

If Alzheimer's disease knocks her down five times, she'll be my Rocky Balboa. I'll be helping her up for round six with my love and devotion, not to see her endure more affliction from the blows of Alzheimer's, but for her to hold on to the *rope of life* so that we could continue loving each other one more round.

33
Afterword

I began writing *Ice and Eyes in the Sun* in 1999 and finished my fortieth draft on March 3, 2012, when I rested a red rose on Fats's casket and softly said my first "goodbye" to her.

I had put down the manuscript stained with teardrops. The 2008 Presidential Election campaign, too, wouldn't let me finish my story, but at the same time it was therapy for me. I love politics, and listening to Chris Matthews' weekly *Hardball*, which is politics squared, is a must like eating cooked rice.

On November 4, 2008, when it was announced, "President-elect Barack Obama will be the new President of the United States of America," it was time to play God, and I did, when my wife became frail and weak: *She will pass soon from this wretched disease*, and I'd end my true story with "Fats died." I envisioned *that* ending would be as forceful as "Jesus wept." Pastor Crooks loved that verse in the Bible, and had made it her sermon many Good Fridays.

"Hollis, 'Jesus wept' is the shortest verse in the bible. If you don't believe me, check John: 11-35."

I never checked, and had no reason to. I attended agnostic and atheist meetings in Fyzabad, and I never checked for verification when atheist John Jules said, "The Jesus story is mythology." I went to pro-religion and anti-religion houses where food was served, and in those houses I thought of the kindness of the host and not of the love of Jesus when I ate. At bedtime when mammy made me say my prayers I thought of the love of Jesus with mammy's prompting. Mammy christened her five children in whatever church our godparents chose. So in mammy's house there were many religions. Necessity molded me to abide by: What you believe in is good for you, and what I believe in is equally good for me.

Once I had solemnly believed Enid would

predecease me before writing this story. But the after-pain of my second prostate surgery when I had suicidal thoughts made me think differently. Discharged from Long Island College Hospital, I went into our basement, and I gathered 10 years of desk diaries in which I had jotted down Enid's habits before and after Alzheimer's. Still I hadn't a clue of what I should say and who, among others, should read my story until I eavesdropped on a passenger's cell-phone conversation on a Downtown Brooklyn bus. Come to think of it, I didn't eavesdrop on him because many Flatbush, Brooklyn, folks talk loudly on their cells.

I couldn't believe what I heard: "I'm sure she has a man. Every Mother's Day in the past she wanted us to hear The Mighty Sparrow in Madison Square Garden and listen to his new calypsos and then go to a hotel. I had to actually drag that woman to go this time. And when we got there, she didn't know what we came to do in that very nice hotel. Could you believe that? I know all of women's tricks. She's saving her energy for...." He whispered.

I wished I could have heard what the other party had said to him. I knew the accent of that Caribbean man, and I wanted to introduce myself to him. But I did not trust his temper. I knew from childhood that I had never won a fight. Their phone conversation was pretty long.

"She can't account for the money I gave her." He toned down. But I could still hear him because I sat in front of him in an almost-empty bus. "She was so hurry to leave me in the hotel and go ...I got up in time and caught that [redacted] sneaking out."

I made two attempts to barge into his conversation when I heard the adjectives for that woman. I wanted to tell him about my dear wife's behavior before I had any suspicion of how advanced her condition was. Not the way he shamelessly linked that woman to infidelity.

I, too, had gotten up from dozing and found Fats tipping out of a Manhattan hotel. When we left for the city, I boasted. "Gail, your mother and I would be spending the night out...A little movie...Dinner...A night for two only...In case of an emergency, we could be reached at...Don't bother, there'll be no emergency...Let your friend from Washington stay in our house tonight only."

If Enid didn't trip on her nightgown, it would have been singles' night for us in Manhattan. I caught her tipping out. I coaxed her to stay. When she fell asleep, I pushed the heavy desk in the room, blocked the door, and slept on the desk. Next morning she enjoyed the free continental breakfast at the hotel.

Here's to Johnny. I hope he reads about Alzheimer's disease and what it does to its victims. Better still, I hope he has already found out. I knew his real name when we got off the bus, but let's just call him Johnny anyhow.

*   *   *   *

My love for Fats was no different from my love for Milly when I came to New York. The only difference is that I married Fats. I remember the day of that strange conversation in bed with Milly.

"Don't try to bullshit me, Lloyd. A woman knows when she wins. And your wife won a long time ago."

Fats waited for me everyday at Fyzabad bus stop when I came from work in San Fernando. I wanted her to be there. My heart fluttered when I got off the bus, but I never kissed her or said "I love you." In New York we met after work and on "hamburger nights." I never kissed her in the street. I loved her but never said so. Now I kiss her everywhere and often, and every night that I put her in bed.

What a difference time, Alzheimer's disease, and prostate cancer make in our lives.

Her Alzheimer's has changed my life, and I hear the echo of Reverend Buxo's words on our wedding day, "For better or for worse...."

For too long I hid my love and affection as if saying "I love you, Fats" was a forbidden subculture. I never heard my father, stepfather, or mother say, "I love you" to each other. As a young boy, I thought my mother's pregnancy was a testament of what is true love: I observed love was given and received in the dark bedroom, and a baby's cry after the unlicensed midwife slapped my brother or sister's bottom was proof that love was practiced. And that's how it should be.

Dr. Francois Elder Thébaud writes in *West African Mental Health Practitioner's Guide*: "Human behavior is a complex phenomenon, resulting from the interaction between innate predispositions, social and psychological factors, some of the latter being unconscious." The doctor speaks of me in his wisdom.

I also fall within the category of the man from Fyzabad who loves his wife. She had faults that kept me away when we were young. I never believed in loving her regardless of her faults when she was lucid. But now I'd move the sky for her.

Ice and Eyes in the Sun is not reeled for fanfare or to showcase my infidelity. Her story is for the understanding of her behavior because of Alzheimer's disease, and the way I coped and am still coping and not letting my "love look away."

Enid and I were vulgar and insular; and, at times, our built-in prejudices and hubris had the upper hand on us. But should anyone take exception to our misgivings, I sincerely apologize. However, I wish people take heed of this advice: Prepare financially and and emotionally for the yeoman task of caregiving that may fall in your laps.

Morpheus, the god of sleep and dreams, hadn't heard of Alzheimer's disease or must have called it by a different name in his kingdom. But as a god he knew of caregiving. He also knew when one loves his spouse, in one's sleep and in one's wake, revelry and feasting would be met in one's path. As Dr. Joanna Haye puts it in her essay, and that's the reason why I employed her, "God or god is good… We cannot change divine intent."

My latest habit is listening to old tapes of Pastor Crooks exhorting her congregation: "Brother Crooks is my dear husband. He is here today to play the organ. He's a good man. "Let us all pray that he comes back next Sunday to play the organ so that we can again say that he's a good man." I laugh aloud at Pastor Crooks's cunning. My wife laughs along with me not knowing the reason for my laughter. So sad.

What a difference time, Alzheimer's disease, and prostate cancer make.

I had my third prostate procedure. My bone scan was negative. On Friday, October 29, 2010, Dr. Rudberg's procedure at Long Island College Hospital was a radical prostatectomy. As the members of his team drifted from my eyes, I thought of Fats as the anesthesia began to put me to sleep. She was the first thing on my mind when I awoke two and a half hours after my operation. And it will always be so with every sunrise and sunset. "Love is more than a feeling, it is commitment," I learned. I didn't have commitment in the beginning, but I'm locked in commitment to the end with my wife, and will prove the race is won in the end.

*   *   *   *

The First Lady of the United States, Michelle Obama, gave her keynote address at Young African

Women Leaders Forum at Regina Mundi Church, Soweto, South Africa, on June 22, 2011. Her address was on the importance of the role of young women leaders on the African Continent and why bullet holes are in Regina Mundi Church. Lloys attended that forum as a guest of Graca Machel, Nelson Mandela's wife. The First Lady and Lloys took pictures. Lloys e-mailed me those pictures. When I received them, I laughed and became emotional at the same time because: If Fats were lucid, she would have bragged, and she would have said, "That is my chil' with the First Lady!" I would have replied, "Yes, Fats, that's your child only because you conceived her without my help. And, furthermore, the word is spelled c-h-i-l-d."

    She would have answered, with gusto, "You went to a vocational school for dunce children… I went to St. Augustine Girls' High, a real school and Brooklyn College. Now you want to teach me how to spell! I am smarter than you, boy. How many times do I have to remind you of that one thing?" That was one of her favorite put-me-down psalms.

    The argument would have begun, and it would have ended with a legato of laughter. She would have thrown herself on the floor; she would have rolled like a ball; and would have reminded me, comically, of my poor days in Fyzabad bush when I ate mangoes for three meals. I miss those "sweet" digs. She loved me from the first day she saw me in Fyzabad Post Office. It took me long to know how deep was her love. But now I know, and she is dead and cannot hear if I say, "I love you truly, Fats."

My habit was to change her wet pampers twice at night, sometimes three times. I changed her pamper 7.12 A.M. on Saturday, February 25, 2012. She looked at me, closed her eyes, and never opened them again. I refused to look when my wife's wrapped body was taken out of **519**, her home that she had flooded with fun and laughter for her children, grandchildren, and me. I wept bitterly.

The church was packed to capacity for her funeral service. I called the members of Divine Truth Assembly to join in with the family to march in. Lloys conducted the service and she called her brothers, sisters, her aunt, Versll, and friends to speak; and they spoke in glowing terms of the deceased. It was gratifying to hear some of the nice things they said of Pastor Enid Cynthia Bain-

Crooks. And our children polished their mother's life with style in their farewell speech.

    Khafra played "Misty" on the keyboard for his Granny. It was one of the tunes he played for her before lifting her in bed. His touch was mournfully beautiful. The late Errol Garner, the composer of "Misty," would have been proud him. As he rose from the keyboard, Lloys said, "Daddy, your turn."I had prepared to play "The Nearness of You," the song that united Fats and me fifty six years ago. But I shook my head. I could not play it. I'd lost my vision with tears.

    I was the last person to leave her grave in Cypress Hills Cemetery on Saturday, March 3, 2012. I spent half an hour with her, felt her presence, said our password for the last time, rested the last rose in my hand on her grave, and whispered, "Good bye, and thank you, Fats, for pollinating our love all these years." I touched her muddy grave twice, and it was as if Fats told me, "Weep no more Blackboy." I felt the raindrops, and I obeyed. I walked in the drizzle slowly to the limousine with Lloys and other mourners who waited on me. The driver looked at me with a blank face and started the engine. The limousine drove off slowly, bumped in potholes, and I admired the flowers on Fats's grave until I could see them no more.

An unexplained peace came over me; I felt very lonely; and wondered what the future holds for me.

About the Author

Lloyd Hollis Crooks is the author of *Grenada Ghost*, fiction, and *Ice and Eyes in the Sun—True Love Comes Late, Sometimes*, which is a true and poignant love story.

Crooks was a civil servant who covered "sensitive" national and international conferences in the Office of the Prime Minister in the Republic of Trinidad and Tobago during the Eric Williams Administration. To name one conference: The United States of America and Trinidad and Tobago Leased Bases Agreement. Crooks was also a court reporter and a Parliament reporter. In New York, he was a partner's secretary in the Wall Street law firm of Sage Gray Todd & Sims. He also worked as a legal secretary at the Wall Street law firm of Sullivan & Cromwell for 18 years before his retirement.

He lives in Brooklyn, New York, and his best hobby is playing jazz on the piano; and he invites his friends to his solo jazz sessions. His other hobby is traversing the streets of Manhattan. He tells me, "Manhattan streets give me rhythm, and a variety of interesting faces reveal their stories in their eyes at the traffic lights; and I pen my thoughts looking into those myriads of eyes; sometimes I can tell the country from which some of those eyes came." His favorite hangout is Times Square and in the company of an astute beggar. The beggar's street address is 42nd Street, between Sixth Avenue and Broadway, and his sign reads: INSULT ME AND PAY ME.

Crooks has seven grown children, but he's just as playful now as when he was a young father and played with his pre-teen children.

Watching his joy as he empties his pockets with the pennies, nickels, dimes, and quarters into the beggar's brown-paper bag as he trash talks with ease with the beggar is the same way he writes literature of pain and hardship with ease. But the paragraph that will follow if he were writing about the injustice in the metropolis will encapsulate 'the struggles and the fortunes of the haves and have-nots. And why he, Crooks, should never find laughter in throwing pennies at a beggar.' He always tells his children, "I'm just one paycheck better than any beggar so it is easy for me to write about dearth because I know what that is when it comes to finding food for the table."

Ice and Eyes in the Sun can be compared with John Bayley's *Elegy for Iris*, a New York Times bestseller.

Crooks, the author, is my father.

Trish-Ellen Jackson

www.ingramcontent.com/pod-product-compliance
Lightning Source LLC
Chambersburg PA
CBHW071645090426
42738CB00009B/1427